LEARN ACOUSTIC GUITAR

Pauric Mather

First Edition - 2014

Revised Editions - 2016 - 2018 - 2020 - 2022

Copyright © Pauric Mather - All Rights Reserved.

No part of this publication may be reproduced in any form or by any means graphic, electronic, or mechanical, including photocopying, recording, taping, or information storage and retrieval systems - without the prior written permission of the author.

ISBN-13: 978-1547245697

ISBN-10: 1547245697

Layout & Design

Hammad Khalid - Malaysia - HMDGFX.COM

Photography

Emma Curtin - Ireland

Translation

Florica Dohan - Ireland

Marco Chu - Australia

Carlos Reyes - Mexico

Andrea Santucci - Italy

InHye Kim - South Korea

Lara von Dehn - Germany

Rafael Mazin Reynoso - USA

Himawari Yamamoto - Japan

Jean-Michel GEORGE - France

Joana Peixoto Meneses - Portugal

If this is your first day learning guitar you're in good company. *All the greats had a first day too - and began a lifetime playing guitar that day.*

YOU CAN BEGIN A LIFETIME PLAYING GUITAR
TODAY!

YOU WILL LEARN

- TO STRUM IN PERFECT TIME
- THE MOST PLAYED RHYTHMS
- THE MOST PLAYED CHORDS
- TO CHANGE CHORDS FAST
- TO READ CHORD BOXES
- TO READ GUITAR TABLATURE

AND MUCH MORE!

CONTENTS

LESSON 1 — 7
- How Not To Play Guitar
- The Best Guitar For You
- Everything You Need
- How To Tune Your Guitar

LESSON 2 — 19
- Start At Perfect
- How To Hold a Guitar Pick
- How To Position Your Chord Hand

LESSON 3 — 27
- How To Read Chord Boxes
- The Best Way To Learn Chords
- 15 Easy Guitar Chords

LESSON 4 — 39
- How To Play Rhythm Guitar
- How To Roll Guitar Rhythms
- 6 Popular Acoustic Guitar Rhythms

LESSON 5 — 47
- 2 New Chords
- How To Change Chords Fast

LESSON 6 — 55

The Spider Exercise
How To Use A Capo
2 New Chords
4 Easy Chord Changes

LESSON 7 — 67

More Easy Chord Changes
3 New Chords
2 Playing Exercises

LESSON 8 — 75

How To Time Guitar Rhythms
4 New Chords
More Easy Chord Changes

LESSON 9 — 91

2 New Chords
4 Popular Chord Sequences
How To Read Guitar Tablature

LESSON 10 — 103

How To Play Fingerstyle Guitar
6 Popular Fingerstyles
50 Most Played Guitar Chords

HOW TO LEARN
GUITAR

The ability to play guitar is *"A Priceless Gift"*. It lets your heart speak, and your imagination roam. Even when words fail, music speaks. And yet, unlike material wealth, once you have it, no one can take it away from you.

The lessons in this book have helped thousands of people to play guitar. They are the most complete, individual and personalised you will ever find. You start simply by knowing what not to do - and also by making sure you have the right guitar to learn on.

From there, it is vital that you follow each lesson step by step. Don't just read them. Personalise and interact with them. Highlight tips that really transform your guitar playing.

MAKE THIS **YOUR OWN BOOK**

Do not skip lessons. The only way they will not work is if you're too eager to move to the next lesson. By taking the time to absorb what you just learned, the quality of your guitar playing will be so much better.

Most importantly, all your practice is pre-planned from start to finish. You know exactly what to work on and won't forget to practice anything. As well as being the key to your success, the "practice programs" keep you on track from start to finish. And you can achieve in weeks, what took many people years to learn.

So Come On Now ... *Pick Up Your Guitar* ... and come with me on *A Truly Unique Musical Journey*.

LESSON 01

- HOW NOT TO PLAY GUITAR
- THE BEST GUITAR FOR YOU
- EVERYTHING YOU NEED
- HOW TO TUNE YOUR GUITAR

LIVE WEBINAR - VIDEO - EMAIL SUPPORT

For all students learning from Pauric Mather guitar books.
Ask questions about anything you need help with.

Email support@pauricmather.com

LESSON 1

HOW **NOT** TO PLAY GUITAR

There are 9 reasons why people fail to learn guitar. Avoid them and you have just about written your own guarantee of success. Here they are;

- Weak fingers
- Bad guitar teachers
- Bad thumb positioning
- Learning music theory
- Learning rhythms badly
- Learning G the wrong way
- Holding a guitar pick badly
- Learning on nylon string guitars
- Holding guitar neck in chord hand

BAD THUMB

If your thumb is badly positioned your guitar will often sound muddy.

If you raise your knuckle, you can play basic chords. But fast chord changing is impossible.

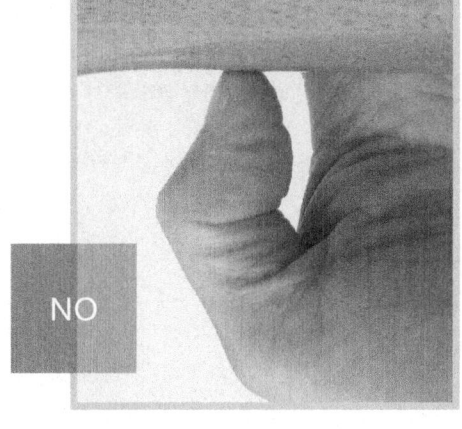

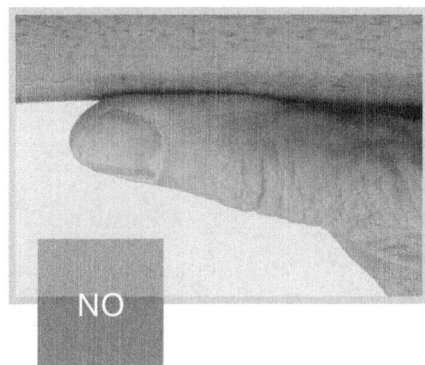

If your thumb falls sideways, It makes it very difficult to change chords quickly, and to play chords up the guitar neck.

 ## BAD HOLD

With a bad grip you can play basic rhythms but you will find advanced rhythms very difficult to perfect.

Learning the G chord as shown below is one of the main reasons why people give up playing guitar. This G only works when you pick each string one by one. But not when you strum all the strings at once.

It sounds muddy. And it can lead to other problems as you try to improve.

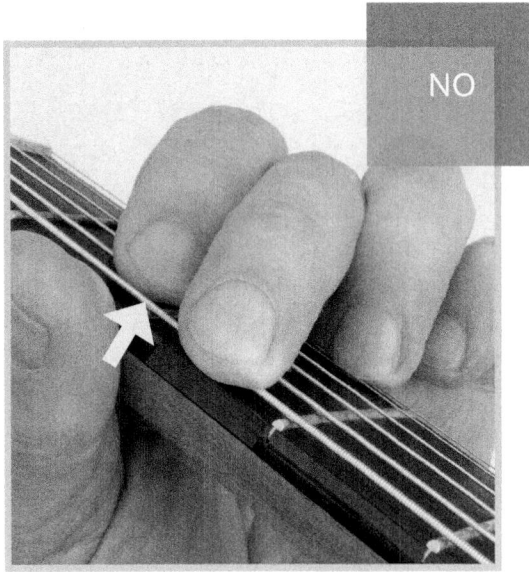

Changing to C and D can be difficult.

You can't add as many bass runs or ornamentation.

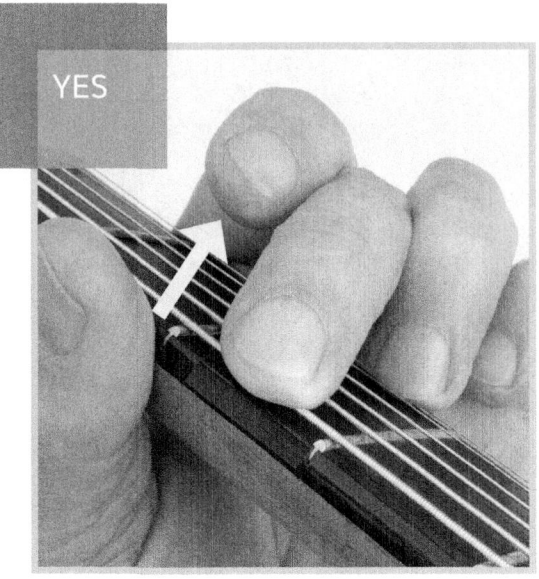

The best way to learn G is more difficult, but only for a few weeks.

After that you have a lifetime of endless possibilities. It is mostly played two ways.

One gives a rich airy sound. The other frees your 1st and 2nd fingers to add more notes, polychords, and bass runs.

Most beginners pull the guitar neck back and crouch out and down to see the strings. Avoid this and you will learn and improve much much faster. And your guitar will be so much easier to play.

Guitar neck pulled back too far

- A faulty set up closes many doors
- It makes chord changing very difficult
- It makes strumming guitar rhythms very difficult
- It also can block the air supply needed to sing well

LESSON 1 | 12

THE BEST GUITAR FOR YOU

If you're a beginner you need to know if you strum better with your right or left hand. The one you write with is almost always the hand you strum a guitar with. If you're not sure try strumming a guitar both ways to see which is most natural.

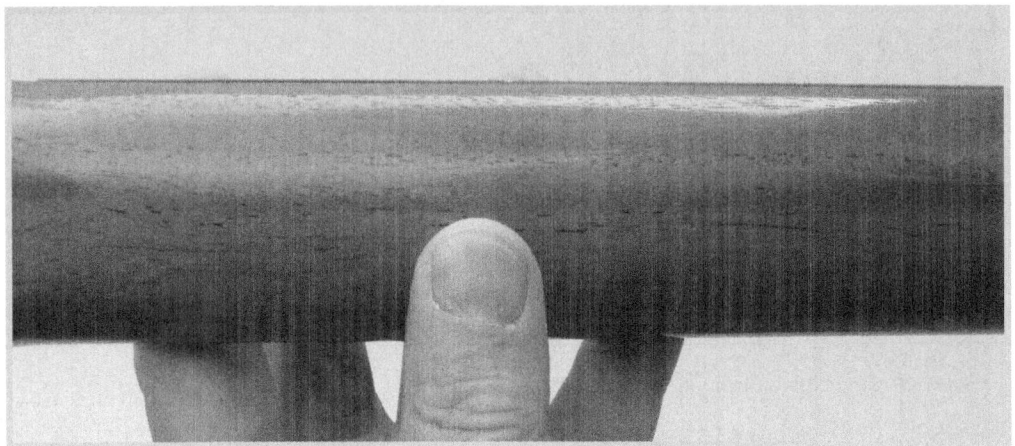

A slim neck

Most professionals play slim neck - steel string - acoustic guitars. So should you (unless you want to play classical guitar).

LESSON 1 | 13

Light gauge strings are easier to play and won't hurt your fingertips too much. By keeping a guitar in a case when not practicing the strings can last for a year or more.

If it's left out they tend to gather dust and need to be replaced often. You can also wipe them after playing.

 # GIRLS

Many of you have smaller body frames than men so it makes more sense to learn on a slim size and slim neck guitar.

As well as being much easier to play, you will be much more comfortable.

14   LESSON 1

EVERYTHING
YOU NEED

 ## GUITAR TUNER

If your guitar has a built-in tuner you do not need to buy one.

A clip on tuner is the easiest to use, especially if you're a beginner.

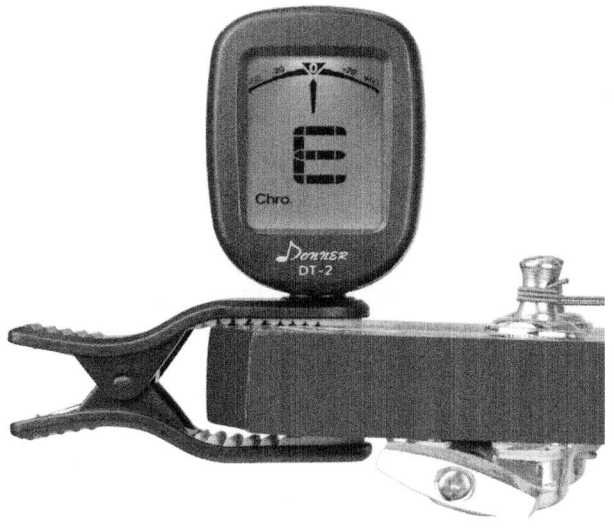

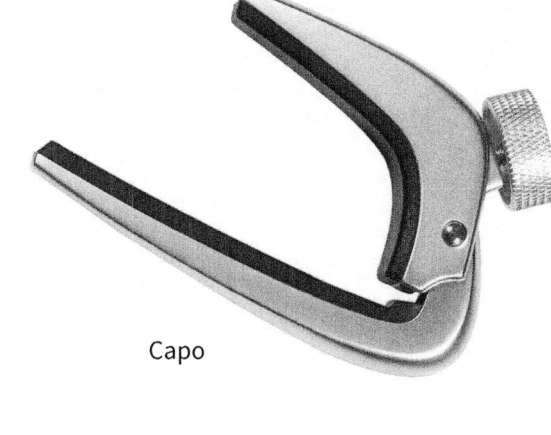

Capo

String Winder

Acoustic Guitar Pick

 # GUITAR BAG

Make sure the zip runs down the side from top to bottom.

It's so much easier to put your guitar into, and take it out of, this type of guitar bag. Also it's better if the bag is well padded.

HOW TO TUNE YOUR GUITAR

Guitar tuners can be tricky for beginners to use. Because they process sound waves you have to pick a string to bring it alive. Then you need to keep sounding the string to keep it responding....and turn the tuning head at the same time to tune the string.

A guitar tuner can process only one sound at a time. If it hears more it doesn't know which sound to process and gets confused.

A clip-on guitar tuner will solve all these problems instantly. They are the most user friendly of all tuners because they only work when attached to the guitar head. So they hear your guitar and nothing else. You can even tune with it in very noisy or crowded areas.

LESSON 1 | 17

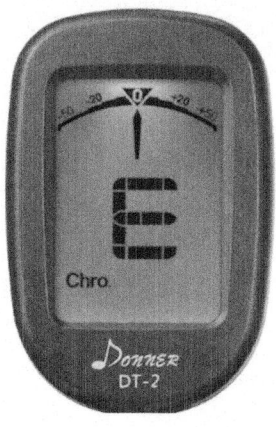

In tune

STRING	NOTE
6th	E
5th	A
4th	D
3rd	G
2nd	B
1st	E

It's not enough to centre a needle or get a green light. The note on your tuner must match the string you are tuning. Sometimes the strings need to be tuned more than once. After tuning it's a good idea to strum a little to settle them. Then tune them again and you're ready to play.

PRACTICE PROGRAM
LESSON 01

- E A D G B E - **17**

- TUNE YOUR GUITAR - **16**

- REREAD HOW NOT TO PLAY GUITAR - **8**

LESSON 02

- START AT PERFECT
- HOW TO HOLD A GUITAR PICK
- HOW TO POSITION YOUR CHORD HAND

LESSON 2

START AT PERFECT

How you set up to play guitar has a huge impact on how quickly you learn. Neglect this vital starting point and it's much more difficult to play.

It only takes a few minutes to learn, but you greatly increase your chances of success.

And if you learn to hold a guitar pick correctly from the start, it's much easier to learn rhythms.

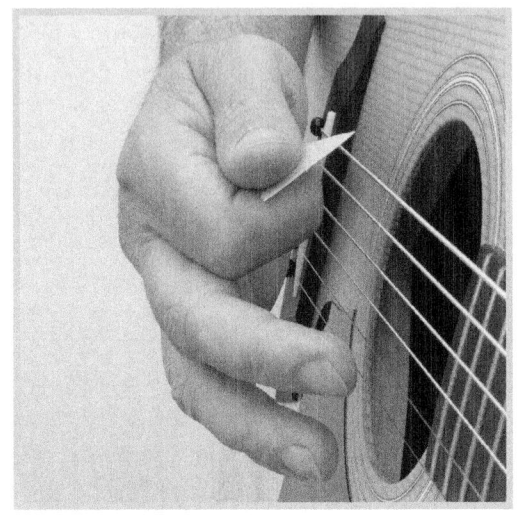

Hold guitar pick correctly

Guitar rests on the same leg as your rhythm hand

Keep the guitar neck angled out about the length of your forearm. This sets your hand in front of you, the same as turning a key in a door. It makes chord changing much easier, and helps to release your natural ability.

Also, the top of the guitar is tilted towards you. Now you can easily see all six strings.

HOW TO HOLD A GUITAR PICK

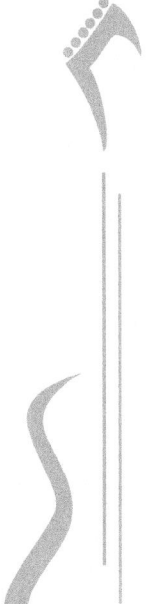

Some people don't like using a guitar pick. They say it slips as soon as they start playing.

But in reality it's their fingers that lose position because they're not holding it the right way.

The learning technique on the next page gives you a great way to hold a guitar pick.

Acoustic guitar pick

LESSON 2 | 23

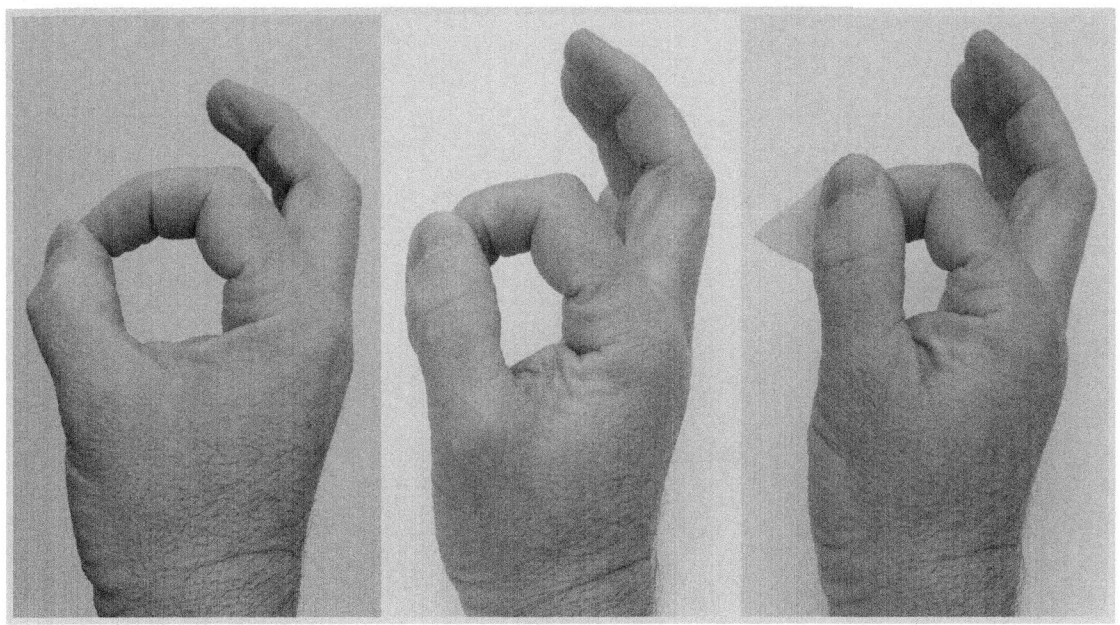

Make
a circle

Slide finger
under thumb

Add
guitar pick

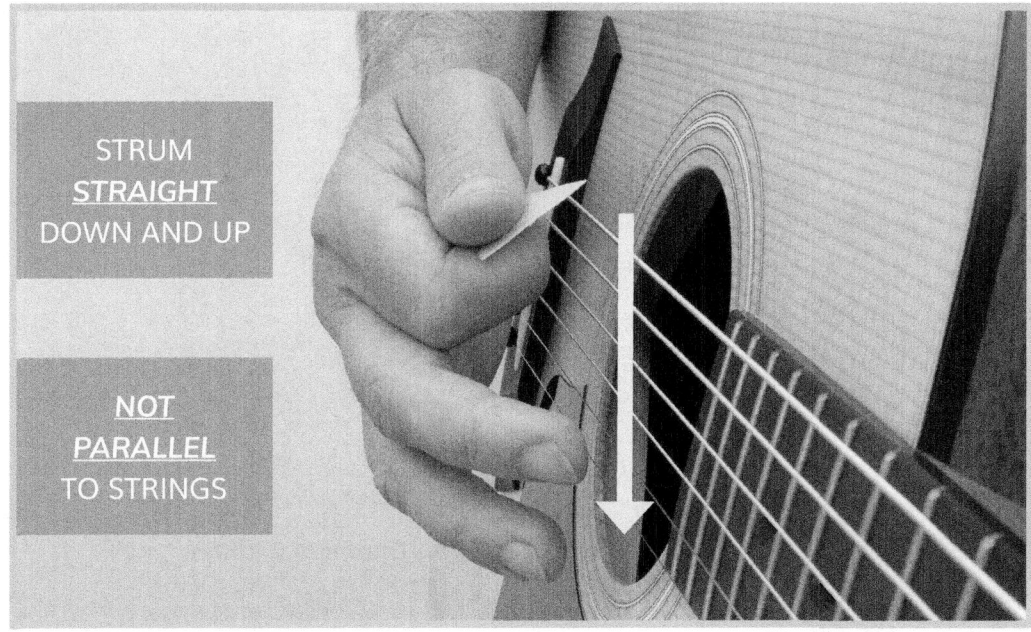

STRUM
STRAIGHT
DOWN AND UP

NOT
PARALLEL
TO STRINGS

LESSON 2

HOW TO POSITION YOUR CHORD HAND

Here is the simplest and best way to position your chord hand every time.

1. Tilt your guitar
2. Position your thumb
3. Then position your fingers

This simple approach makes it much easier to learn guitar chords.

And it's easier to speed up your chord changing too, which is the great secret of playing guitar.

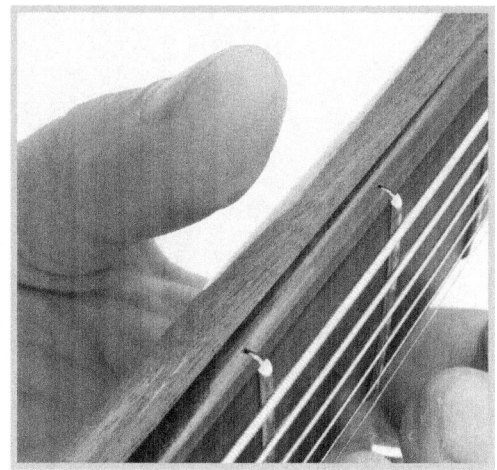

Thumb first - Then fingers

LESSON 2 | 25

 ## TILT YOUR GUITAR

Tilting makes learning chords so much easier. The guitar is now doing some of the work for you. It also helps to produce a good sound.

 ## POSITION YOUR THUMB

1. Thumb on top for open chords
2. Thumb low and centred for barre chords

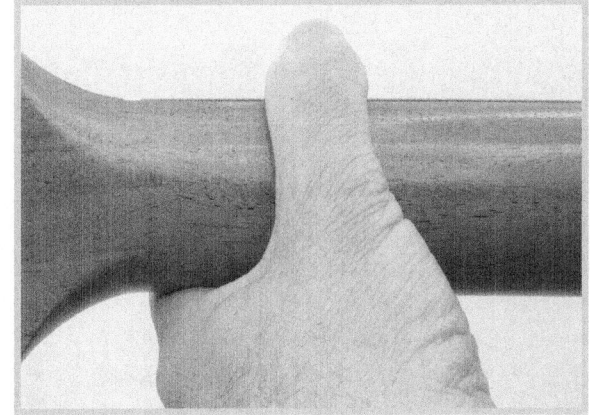

 ## POSITION YOUR FINGERS

The simple 3 step approach here is technically perfect and exactly as played by top guitarists.

It can help you achieve in weeks, what many people took years to learn.

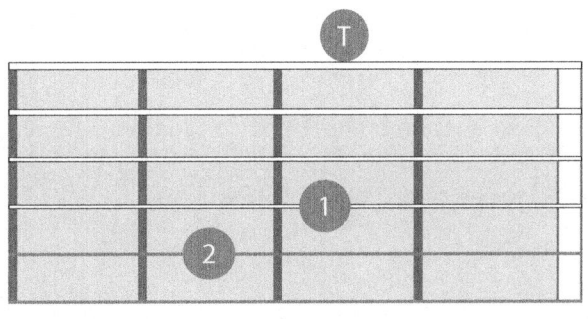

LESSON 2

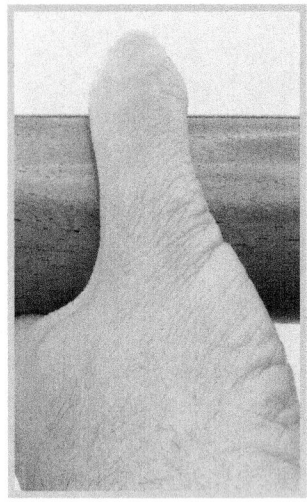
Open chords

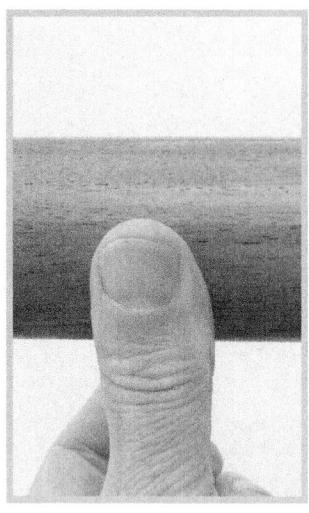
Barre chords

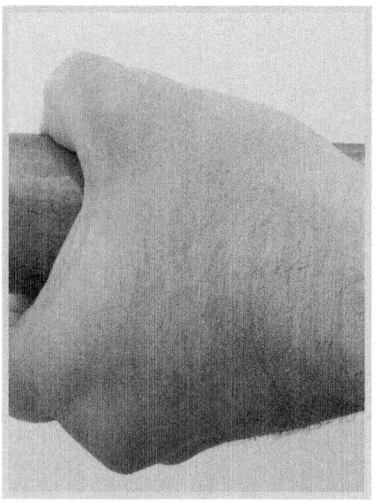
Other chords

THE SECRET

Here is one of the great secrets of playing guitar. In fact without it, nothing is possible.

If you watch any great guitarist, in any style of music, anywhere in the world you'll see *"The Guitar Triangle"*.

- Makes room for fingers to move
- Lets you play with your fingertips
- Prevents knuckles from collapsing
- Makes chord changing easier

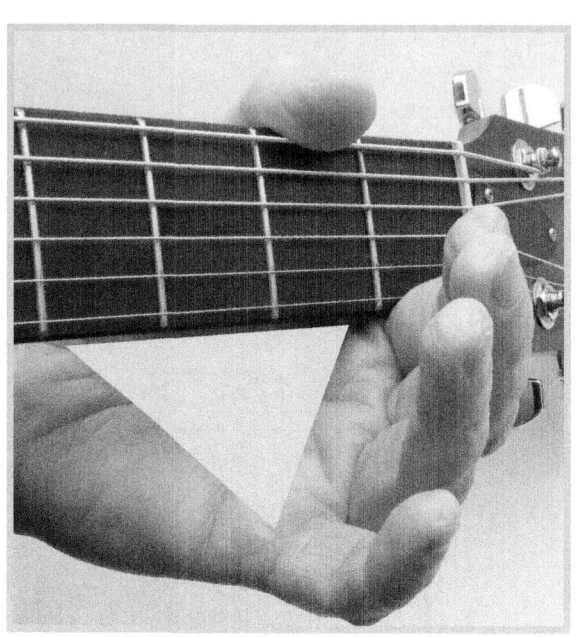
Open chords

LESSON 03

- HOW TO READ CHORD BOXES
- THE BEST WAY TO LEARN CHORDS
- 15 EASY GUITAR CHORDS

28 | **LESSON 3**

HOW TO READ
CHORD BOXES

Chord boxes are hugely helpful if you're an experienced guitarist. But because they only show you the front of the guitar neck, They do not work for most beginners.

However, if you're a beginner the secret is to combine *"The 3 Step Approach"* (Page 25) with the chord box.

Now they're much easier to follow - and save you time.

- **T** — Thumb
- **1** — 1st Finger
- **2** — 2nd Finger
- **3** — 3rd Finger
- **4** — 4th Finger

LESSON 3 | 29

String does *NOT* sound

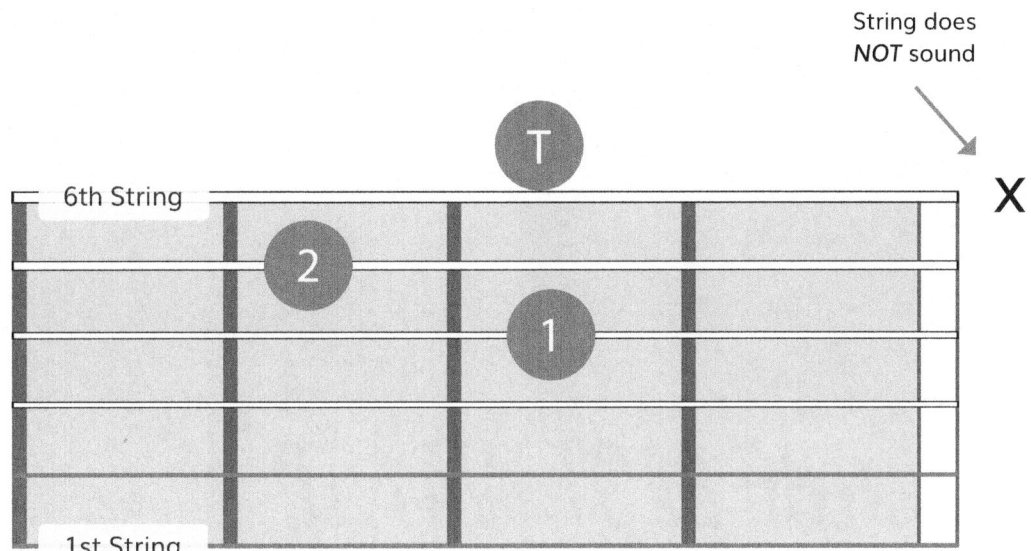

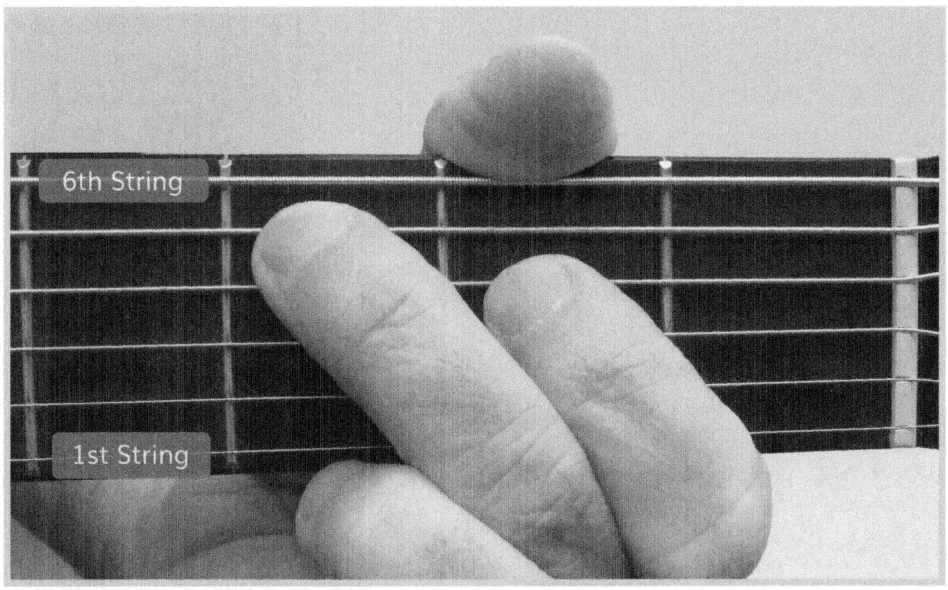

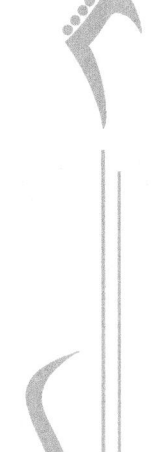

THE BEST WAY TO LEARN CHORDS

The absolute best way to learn guitar chords is to practice a sequence of 3 or 4 chords at a time. And with your chord hand only. Once you get to know the chords you can then add your rhythm hand.

As well as learning new chords, this helps to speed up your chord changes (the bit between them). Whether you're a beginner or professional, D is D and G is G. But the professional is much faster between chords.

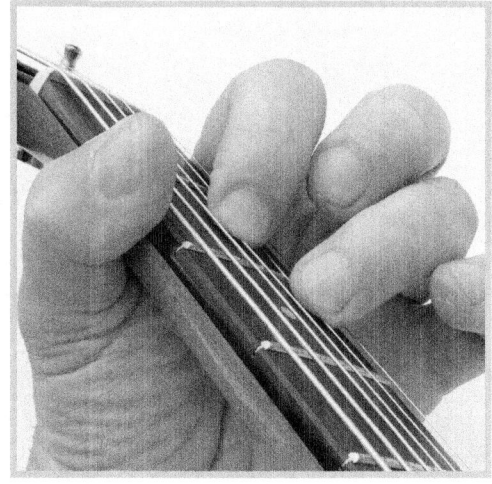

Players' view

15 EASY GUITAR CHORDS

15 Easy Guitar Chords — 32

Em

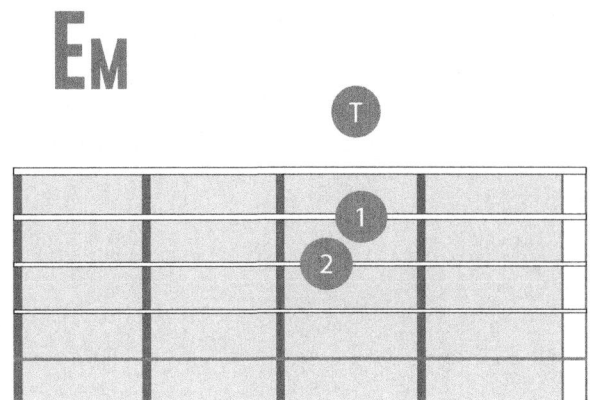
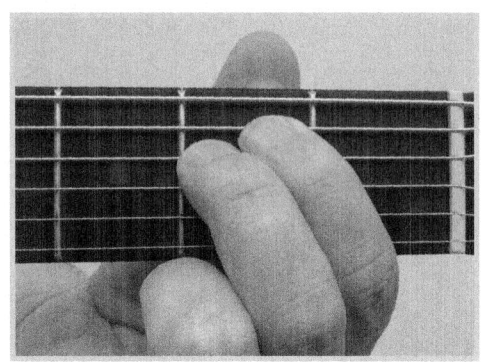

Cmaj7

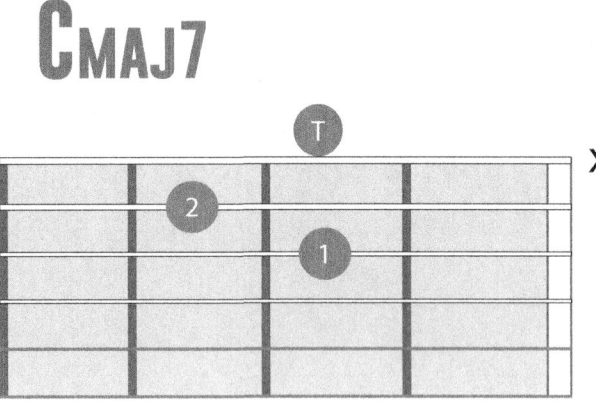
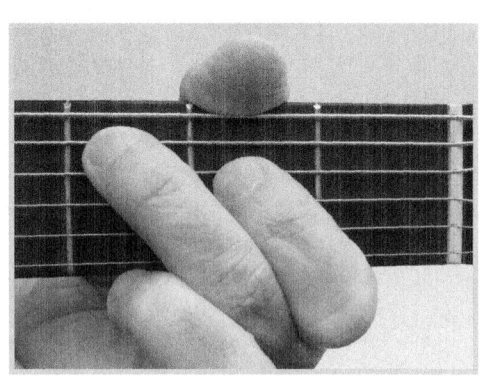

G6

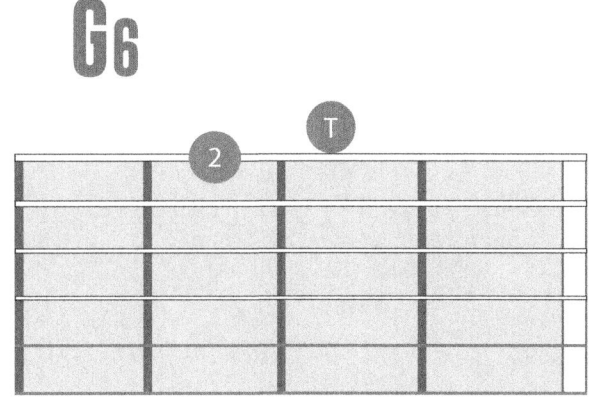
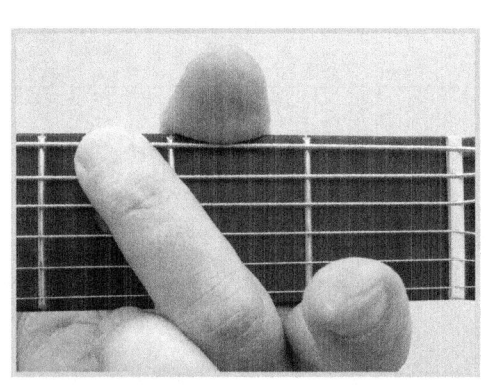

15 Easy Guitar Chords | 33

F# *EASY*

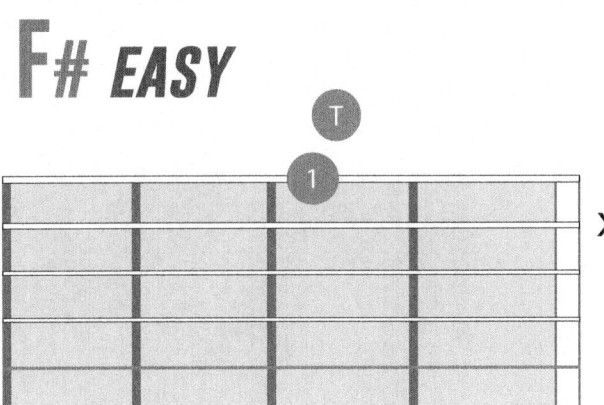
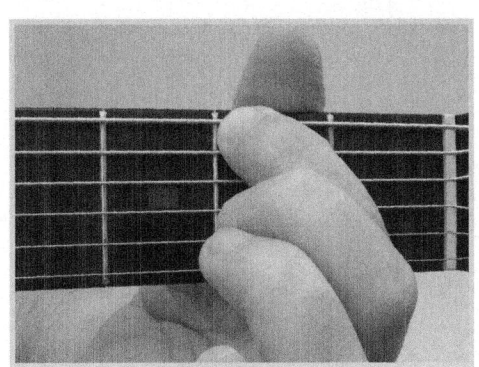

A2

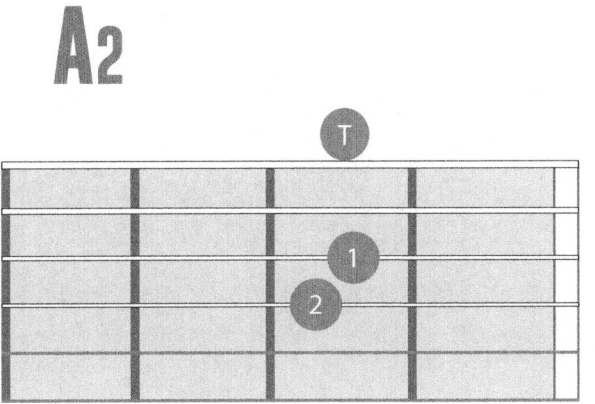
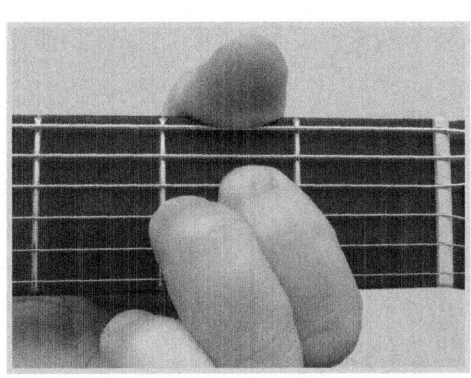

G *EASY*

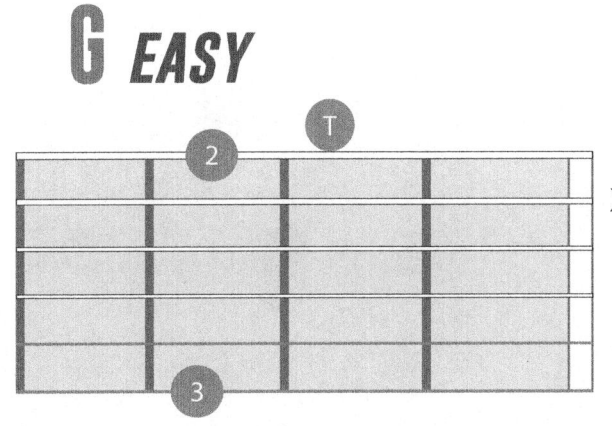
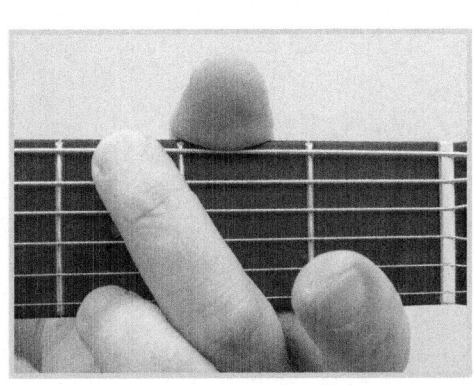

15 Easy Guitar Chords | 34

D2

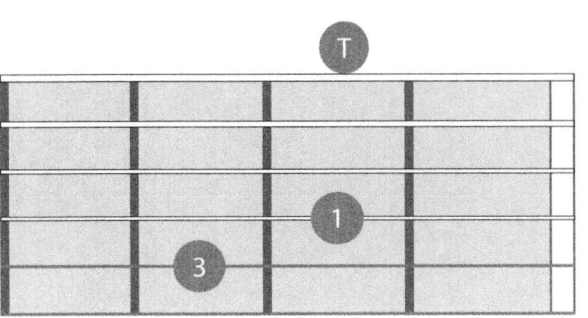
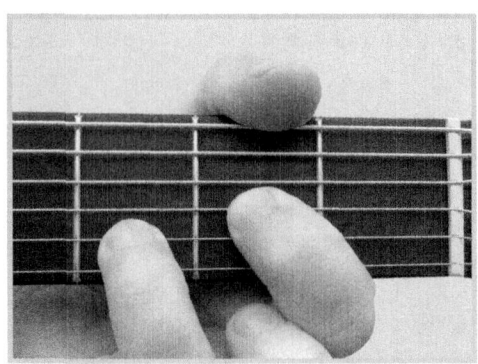

Dmaj9

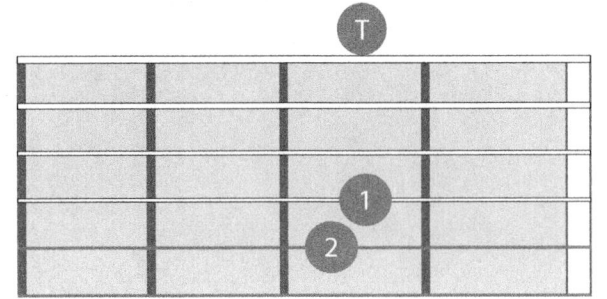
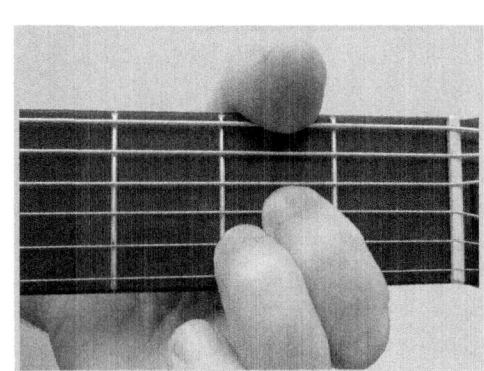

Fmaj7

4TH FRET

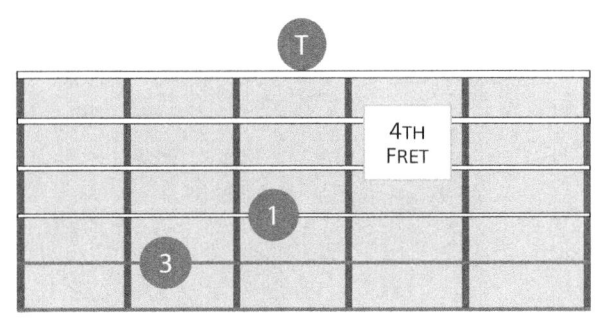
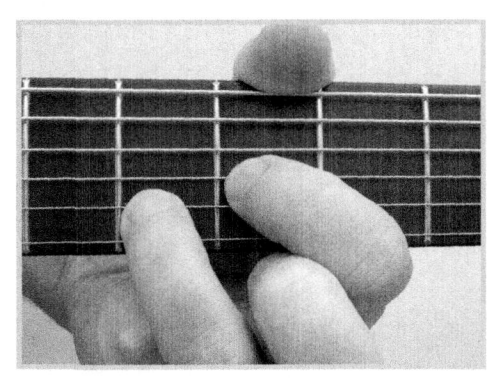

15 Easy Guitar Chords | 35

Em7

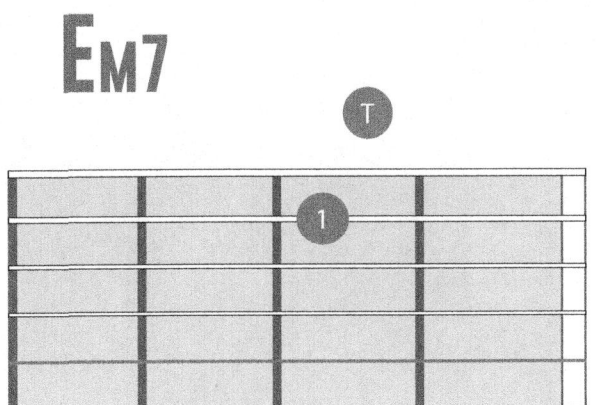
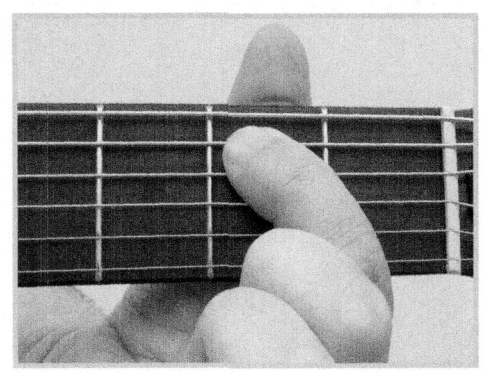

E7

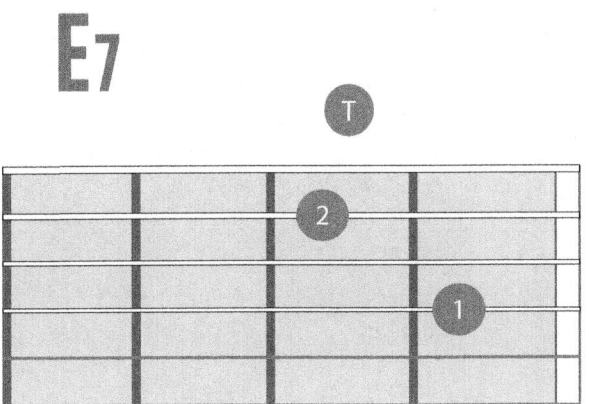
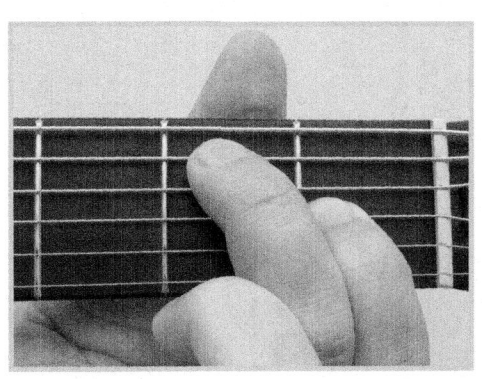

Am7

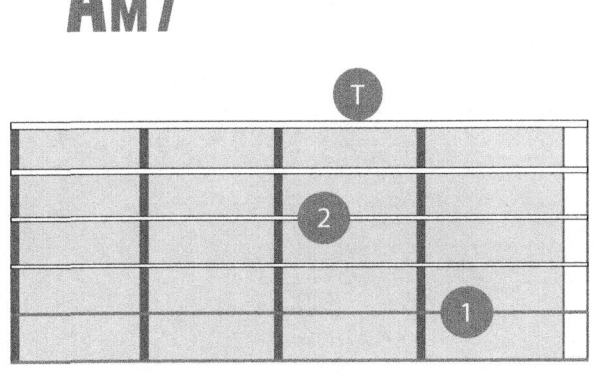
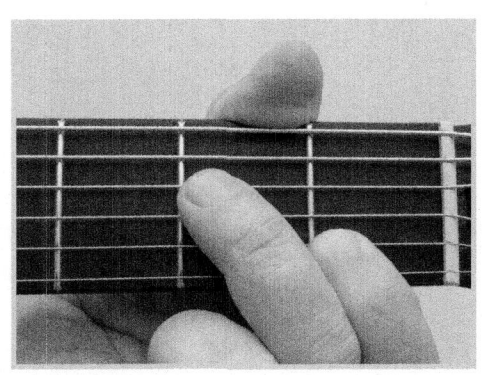

15 Easy Guitar Chords   36

D7sus2

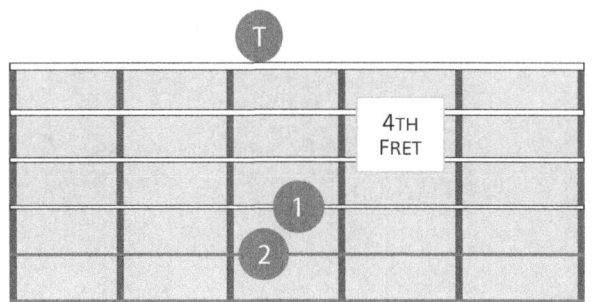

D/E

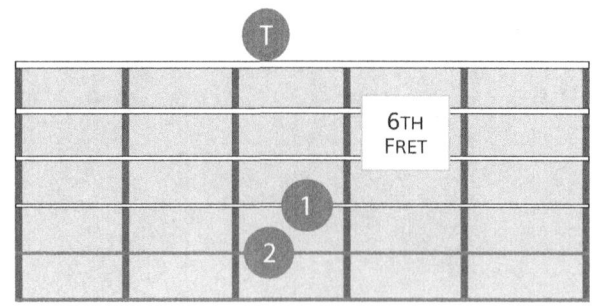
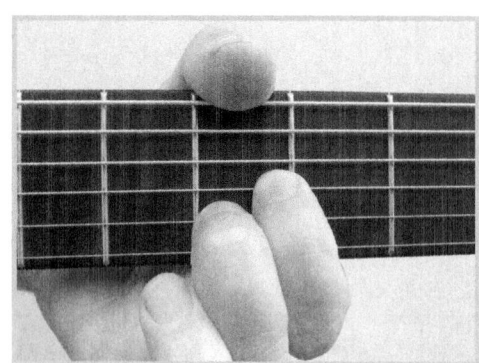

Amaj7

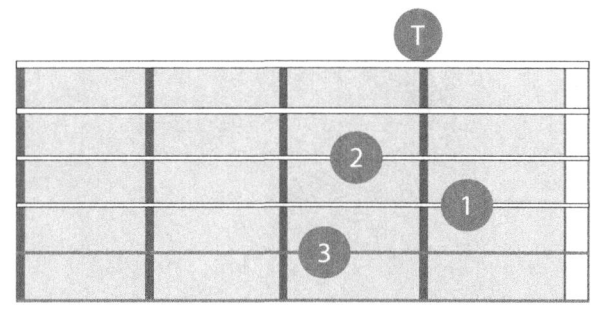
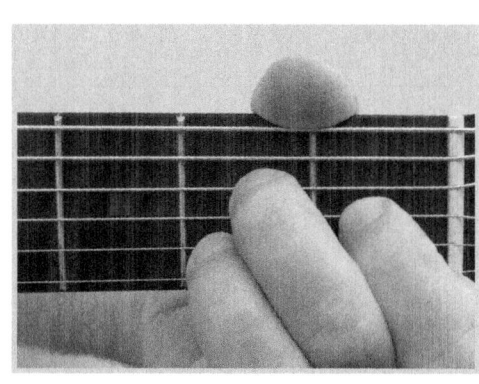

LESSON 3 | **37**

🎸 PLAYING EXERCISE 1

Keep repeating this chord sequence

Em - Page 32

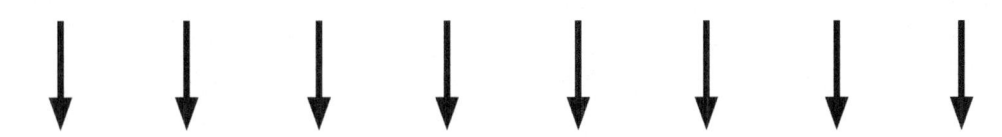

↓ ↓ ↓ ↓ ↓ ↓ ↓ ↓

Cmaj7 - Page 32

↓ ↓ ↓ ↓ ↓ ↓ ↓ ↓

G6 - Page 32

↓ ↓ ↓ ↓ ↓ ↓ ↓ ↓

F# - Page 33

↓ ↓ ↓ ↓ ↓ ↓ ↓ ↓

🎸 SONG EXAMPLE

Zombie - The Cranberries

PRACTICE PROGRAM
LESSON 03

- TUNE YOUR GUITAR - **16**
- HOLD A GUITAR PICK - **23**
- 2 NEW CHORDS - **32-36**
- PLAYING EXERCISE - **37**

LESSON 04

- HOW TO PLAY RHYTHM GUITAR
- HOW TO ROLL GUITAR RHYTHMS
- 6 POPULAR ACOUSTIC GUITAR RHYTHMS

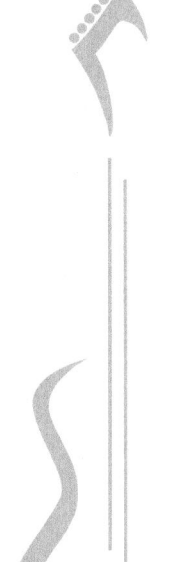

HOW TO PLAY RHYTHM GUITAR

The quickest way to master guitar rhythms is to mute the strings with your chord hand. Now you don't have the pressure of trying to play a song at the same time.

Strumming from over the soundhole gives you a smoother sound. And because the strings seem to bend easier the pick is less lightly to slip.

Some guitarists don't use a pick at all. Instead they strum with their thumb (downstrokes) and 1st finger (upstrokes), or their first finger only for up and down strokes.

Mute the strings

PLAY FROM YOUR SHOULDERS

DOWNSTROKE

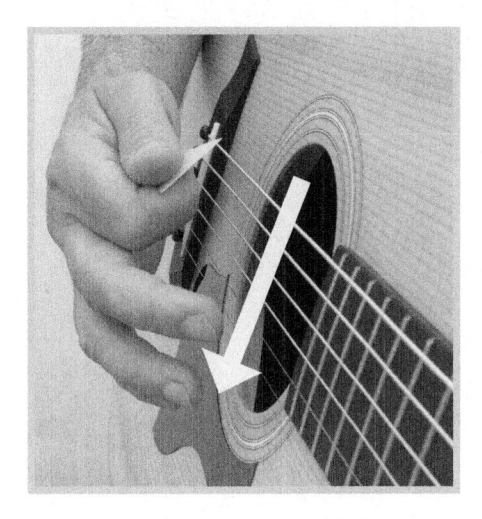

↓ Strum Down
Sound The Strings

↓ Strum Down
Miss The Strings

Plectrum pointed *UP*
Strum 6 strings or less

UPSTROKE

↑ Strum Up
Sound The Strings

↑ Strum Up
Miss The Strings

Plectrum pointed *DOWN*
Strum bottom 4 strings or less

HOW TO ROLL GUITAR RHYTHMS

To strum on time you need to softly roll your rhythms. It is the great key to good sound and perfect timing. Even though there are thousands of different sounding rhythms, there is only one pattern for them all. Here it is.

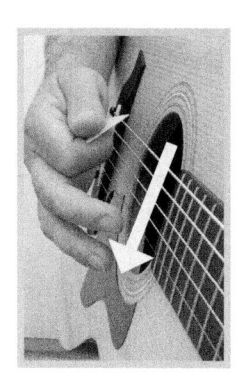

| Down | Up | Down | Up |

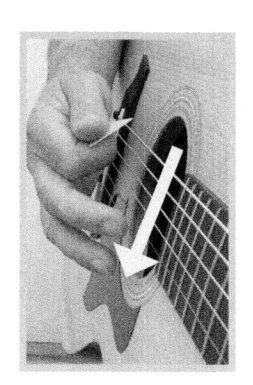

LESSON 4 — 43

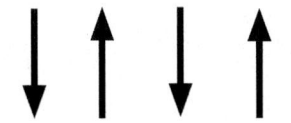

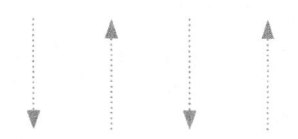

BLACK Arrows - Strum The Strings

GREY Arrows - Miss The Strings

Once a song starts can you feel how it rolls along? It doesn't start stop start stop. To do this on guitar your hand must have a down up down up non stop rolling movement.

In many guitar lessons, someone trying to teach you will say go down down down down. This is very misleading for many people. If I do four downstrokes in a row my hand will hit the ground.

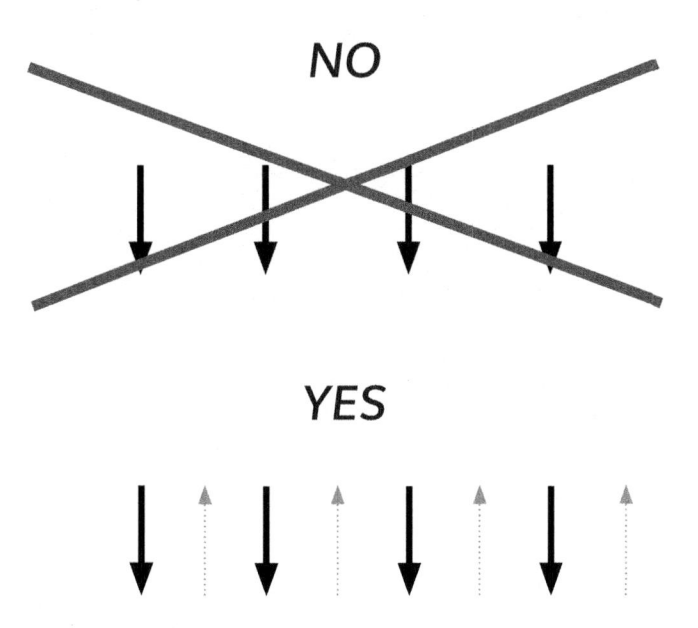

NO

YES

To do four downstrokes:

- You must also do upstrokes between them
- You continually roll your arm / wrist up and down
- But your audience only hears the black arrows

LESSON 4 | 44

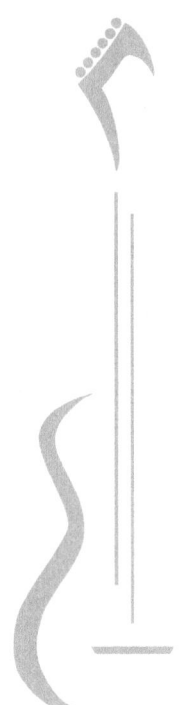

6 POPULAR ACOUSTIC GUITAR RHYTHMS

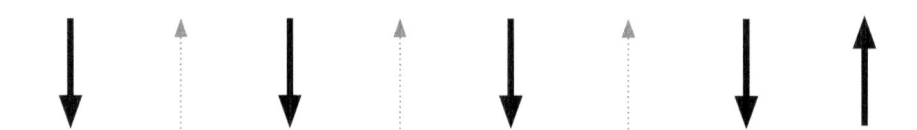

Rhythm 1

↓ ↑ ↓ ↑ ↓ ↑ ↓ ↑

Rhythm 2

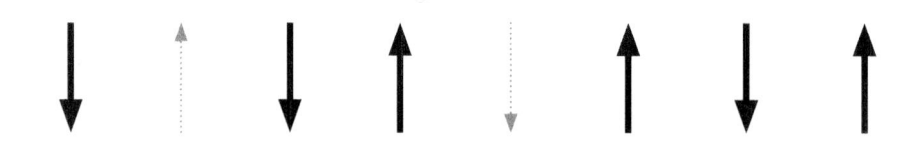

↓ ↑ ↓ ↑ ↑ ↑ ↓ ↑

Rhythm 3

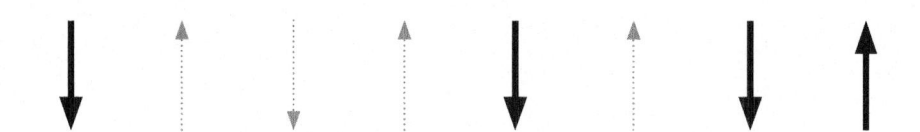

Rhythm 4

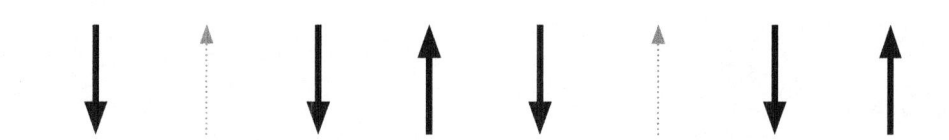

Rhythm 5

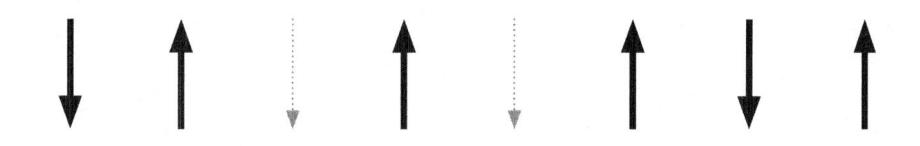

Rhythm 6

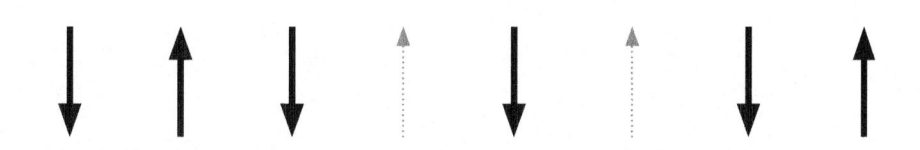

PRACTICE PROGRAM
LESSON 04

- TUNE YOUR GUITAR - **16**
- PLAYING EXERCISE - **37**
- GUITAR RHYTHMS - **44-45**
- 2 NEW CHORDS - **32-36**

LESSON 05

- 3 NEW CHORDS
- HOW TO CHANGE CHORDS FAST

E_M

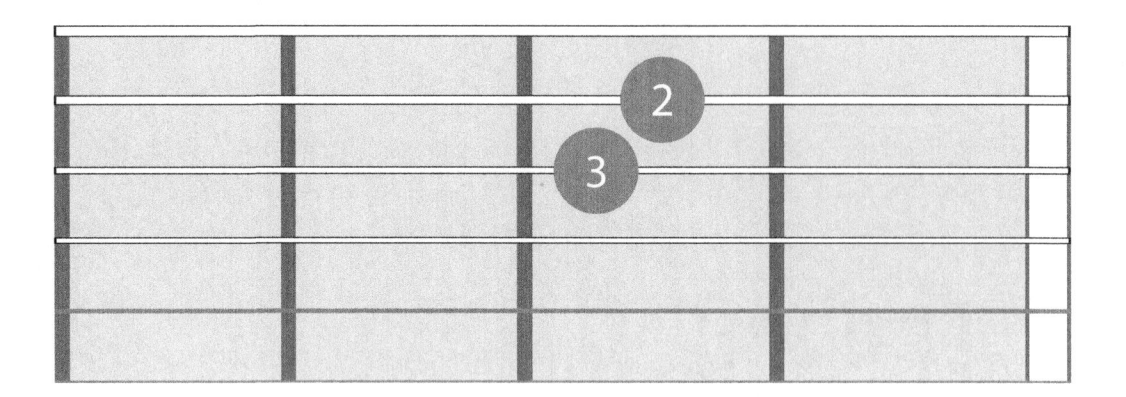

- Thumb not touching 6th string
- Can also be played with 1st and 2nd finger
- Strum 6 strings - All 6 sound

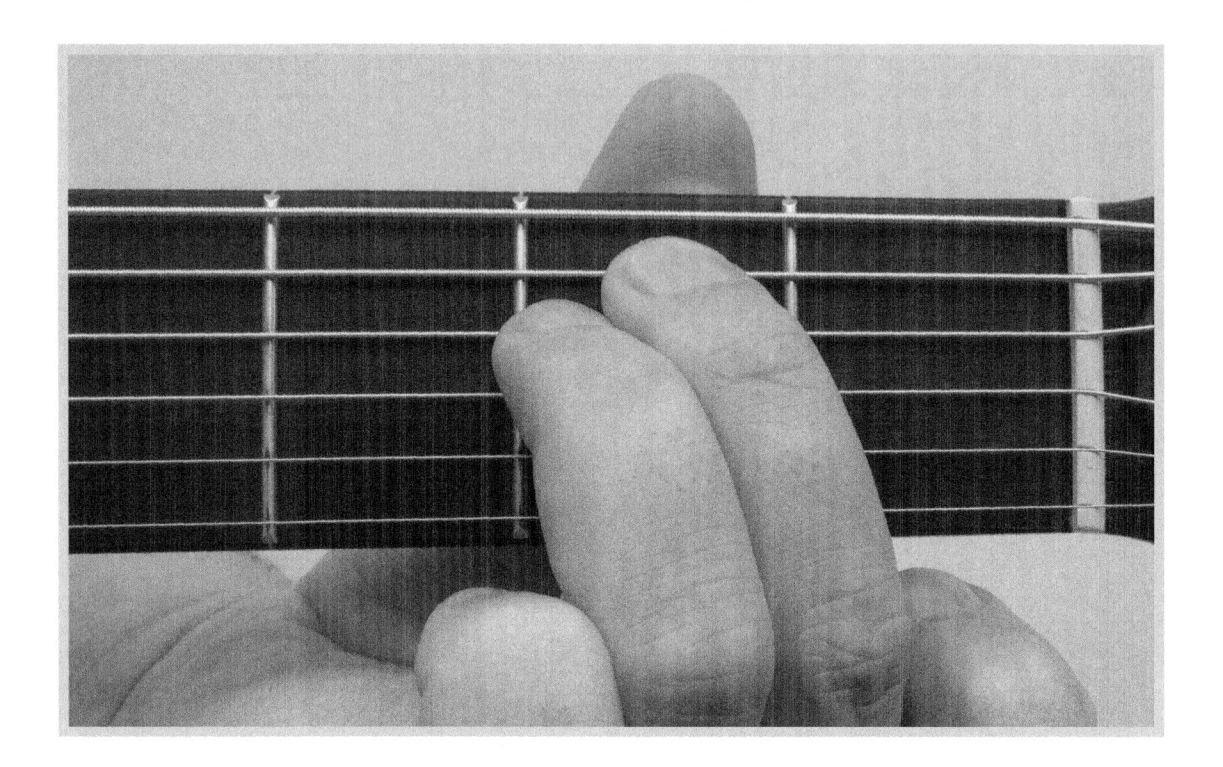

E7sus4

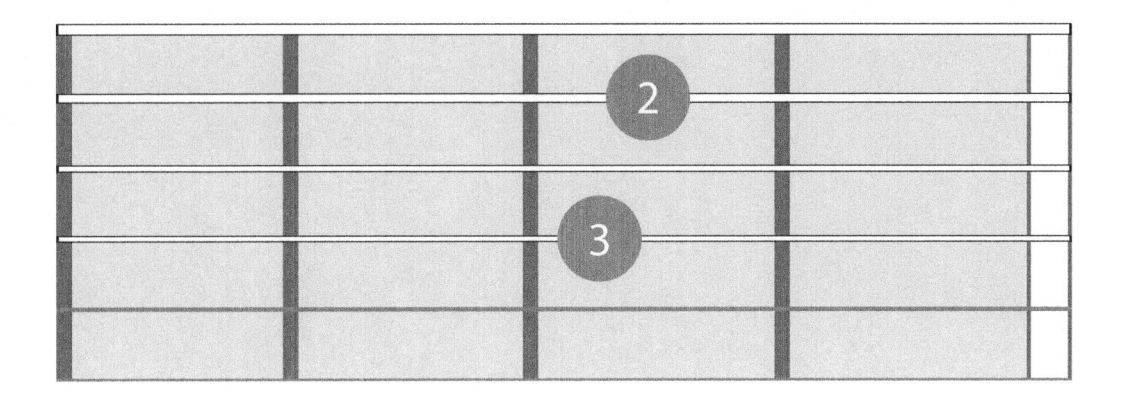

- Thumb not touching 6th string
- Can also be played with 1st and 2nd finger
- Strum 6 strings - All 6 sound

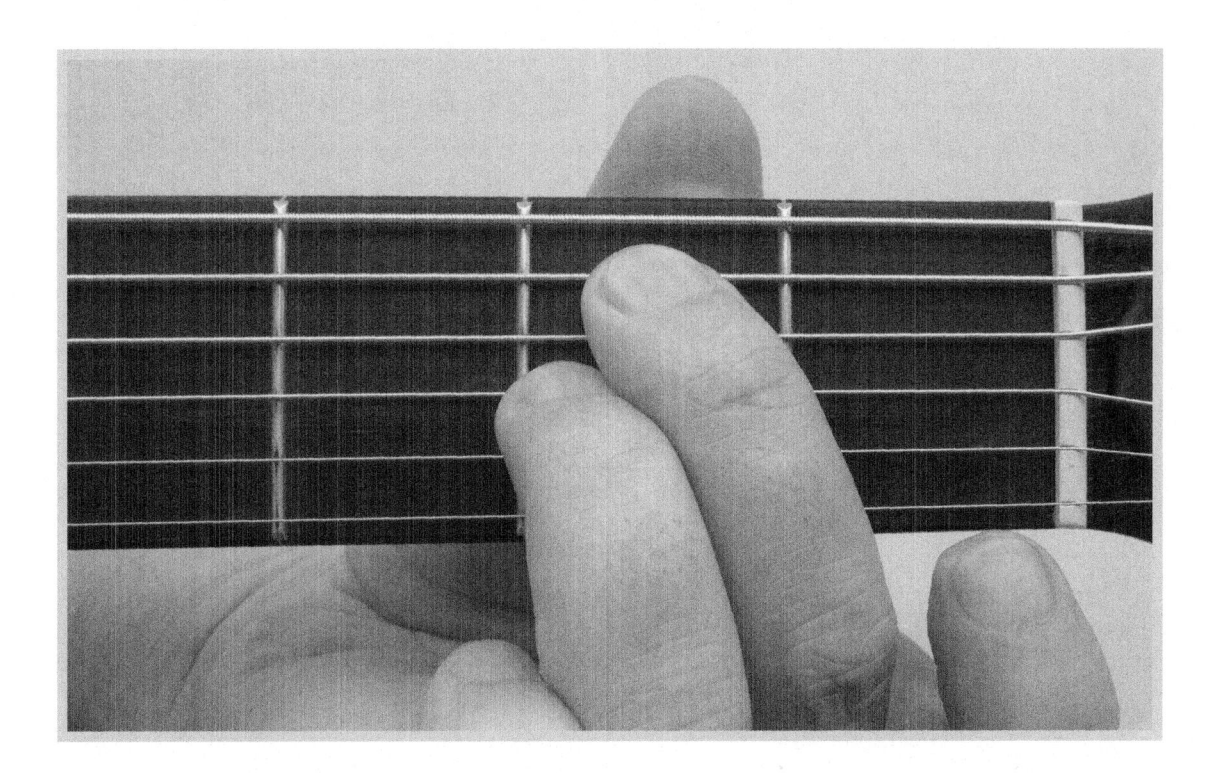

LESSON 5

HOW TO CHANGE CHORDS FAST

When a finger is in the same position for a sequence of two or more chords you don't need to move it.

It's called a pivot finger. Just keep it pressed down and pivot around it.

Most easy chord changes have a pivot finger. Difficult ones don't. Learning guitar is much easier if you practice pivot finger changes first.

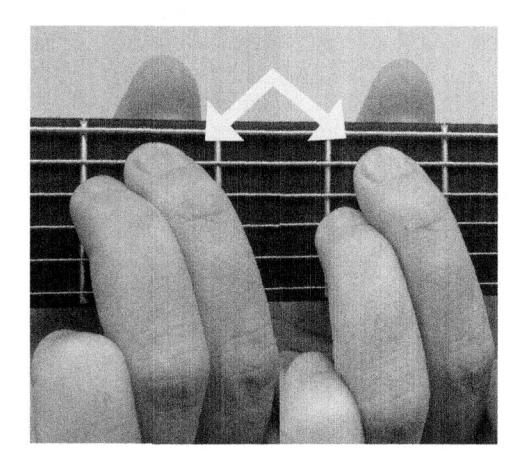

LESSON 5 | **51**

🎸 PLAYING TIP

To change chords well, start moving your fingers in the direction of the new chord, during the last upstroke of your present chord (Em7).

If you don't do this you will have a muddy sound at the start of the next chord you play.

Get it right and two things happen;

1. The chord change is easier
2. The sound Is much clearer

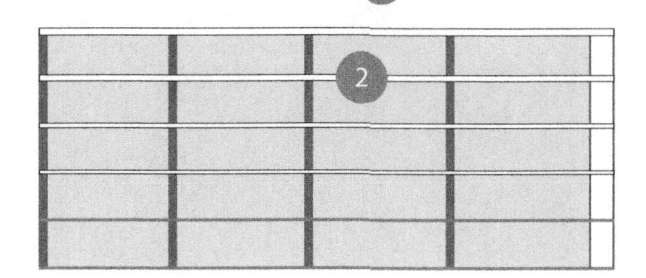

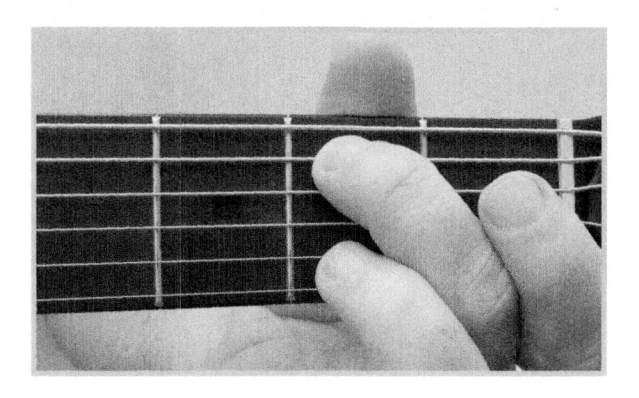

Lift 3rd finger

Em

E7sus4

Lift 3rd finger

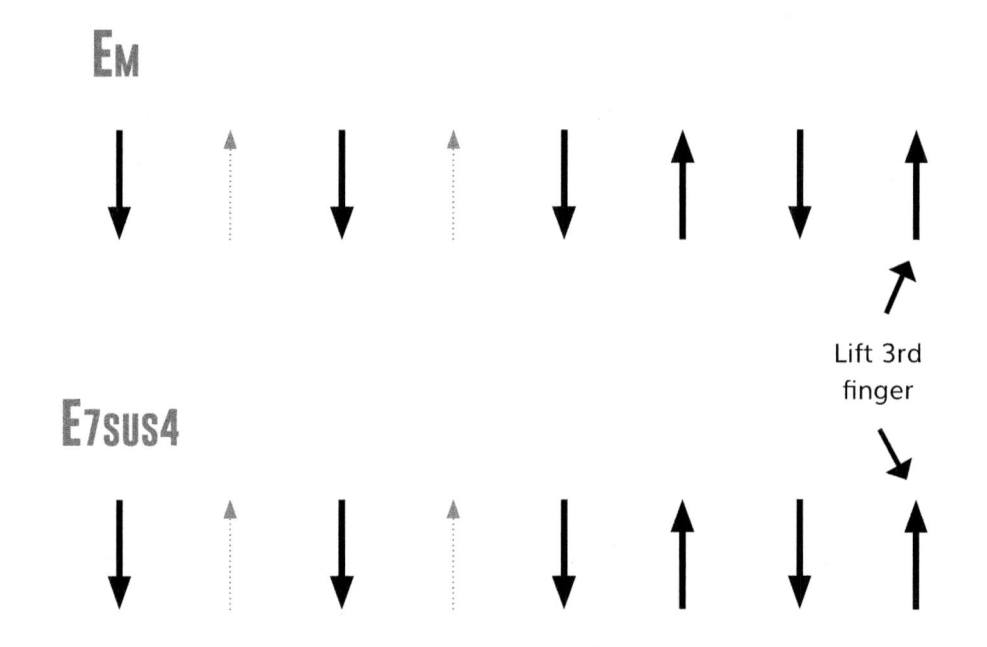

LESSON 5

🎸 PLAYING EXERCISE 2
Keep repeating this chord sequence

Em - Page 48

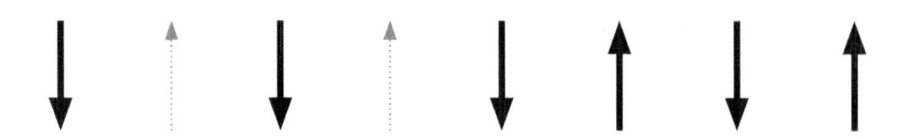

↓ ↑ ↓ ↑ ↓ ↑ ↓ ↑

E7sus4 - Page 49

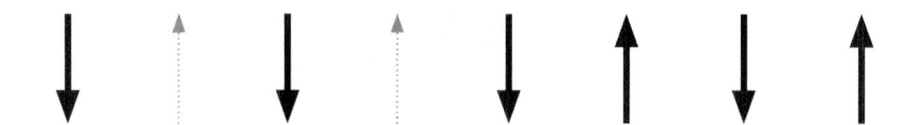

↓ ↑ ↓ ↑ ↓ ↑ ↓ ↑

Em

↓ ↑ ↓ ↑ ↓ ↑ ↓ ↑

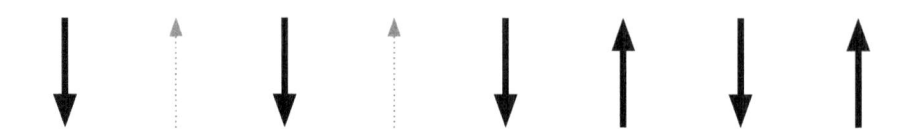

E7sus4

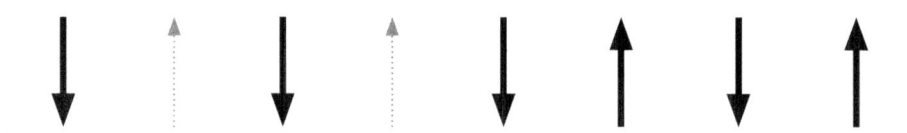

↓ ↑ ↓ ↑ ↓ ↑ ↓ ↑

🎸 SONG EXAMPLE
A Horse With No Name - America

E

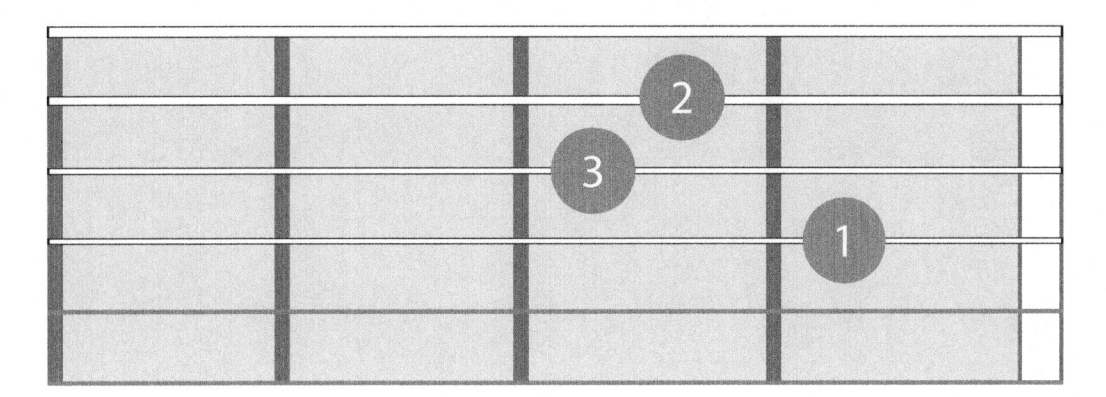

- Thumb not touching 6th string
- 1st finger in corner of fret
- Strum 6 strings - All 6 sound

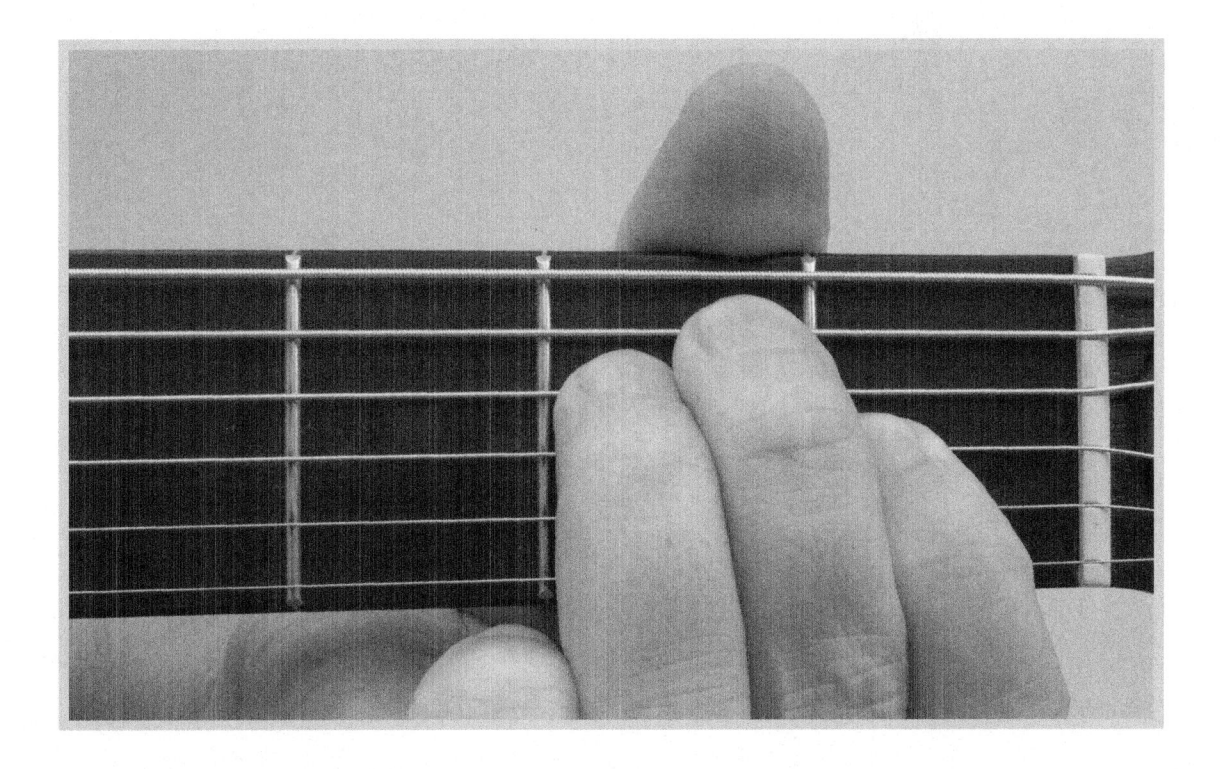

LESSON 5

PRACTICE PROGRAM LESSON 05

- TUNE YOUR GUITAR - **16**
- PLAYING EXERCISE - **37**
- GUITAR RHYTHMS - **44-45**
- CHORD CHANGING - **51**

LESSON 06

- THE SPIDER EXERCISE
- HOW TO USE A CAPO
- 2 NEW CHORDS
- 4 EASY CHORD CHANGES

LESSON 6

THE SPIDER EXERCISE

If you're a beginner your fingertips are too soft to produce clear sound. It usually takes about three weeks for them to harden. Secondly you need four skilled fingers. This exercise will help you to quickly upskill and strengthen all your fingers.

In everyday life you use your thumb and first two fingers for most activities. The 3rd and 4th are seldom used except maybe for typing or playing a piano. Even then you're only lightly touching the keys. Pressing guitar strings is very demanding on all four of your fingers.

STEP 1

Move 1st finger to the 5th string 1st fret

STEP 2

Move 2nd finger to the 5th string 2nd fret

STEP 3

Move 3rd finger to the 5th string 3rd fret

STEP 4

Move 4th finger to the 5th string 4th fret

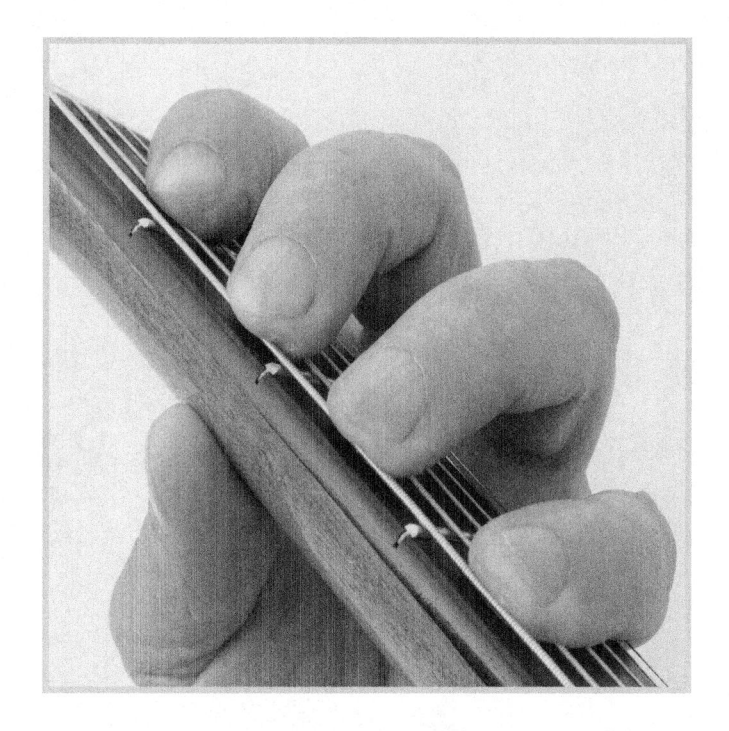

- Place 4 fingers on the 6th string
- One finger in each fret
- Move one finger at a time

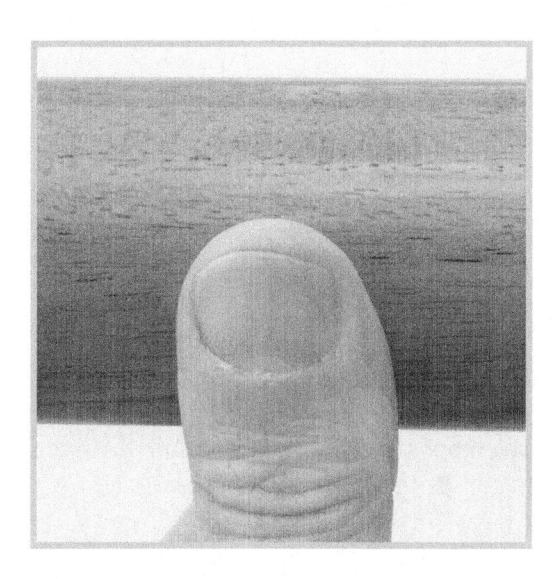

You'll find it quite difficult to move the third finger on its own. Because it's still too weak to play guitar, you might have to use your other hand to move it.

Each time you do this exercise you're a step closer to playing guitar really well.

1

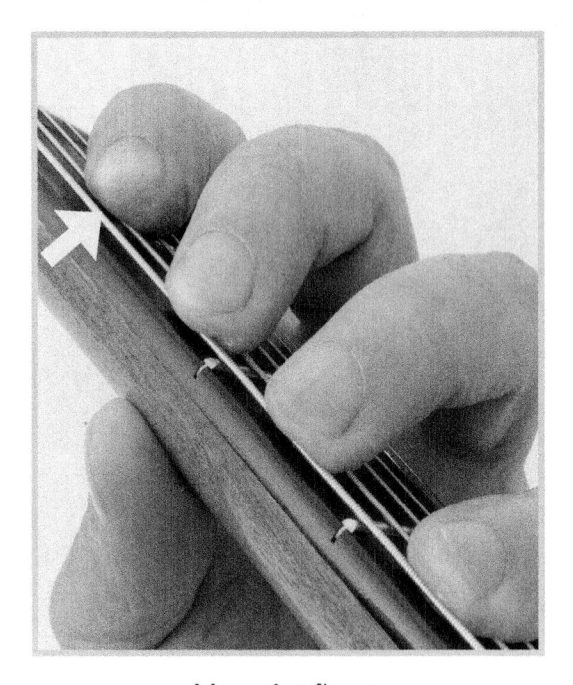

Move 1st finger

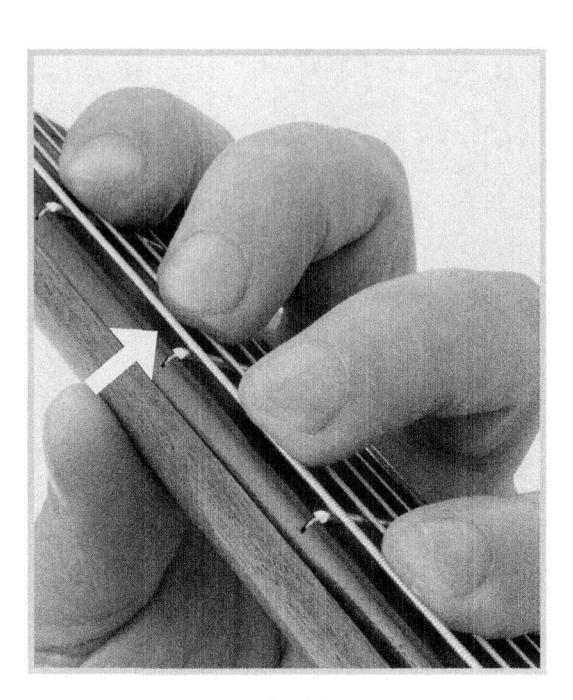

2

Move 2nd finger

CRAMP

Do you feel cramp during this exercise? Don't worry. It's quite normal. Rest your hand until you feel ready to start again. Once your hand is strong it won't cramp anymore.

This exercise really exposes any weakness in your chord hand and fingers in relation to playing guitar. But it's also the solution.

3

4

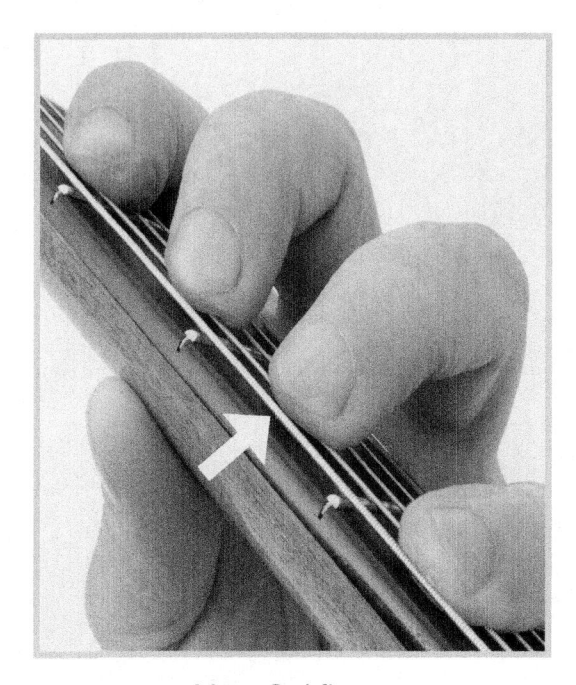

Move 3rd finger

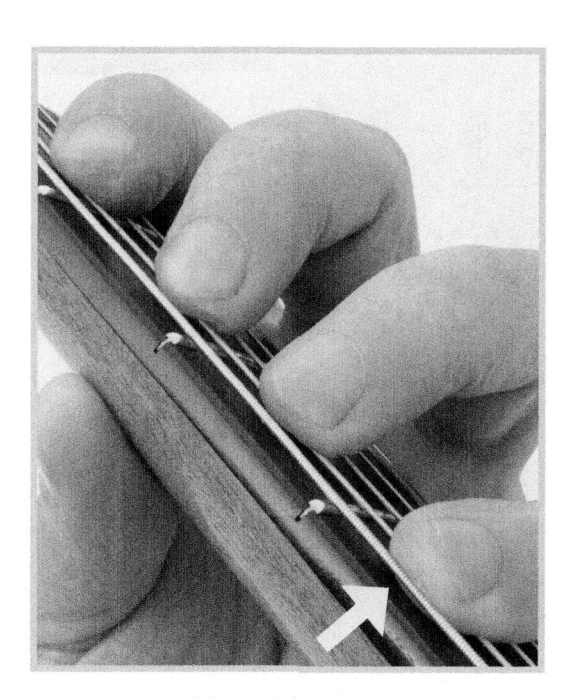

Move 4th finger

- Once you arrive at the finish you can practice back up one finger at a time.

- Start with the 1st finger up one string, then the 2nd finger up one string, then the 3rd and so on.

- Keep going until all four fingers are back on the sixth string. You will find it much easier going back up.

HOW TO USE A CAPO

A capo can be placed on up to ten frets. Even though you play with the same chord positions, you get a different set of sounds for each fret that the capo is on.

Also the guitar should be pitched to the vocalist in order to retain the quality of their voice.

LESSON 6 | 61

If a song suits your voice that's great. If it doesn't, try putting a capo on the 1st fret.

All you have to do is play the same chord sequence again and the song is in a higher key.

If this position suits your voice that's great. If not you can move it up or down as many frets as you like until it suits.

Capo on 1st fret

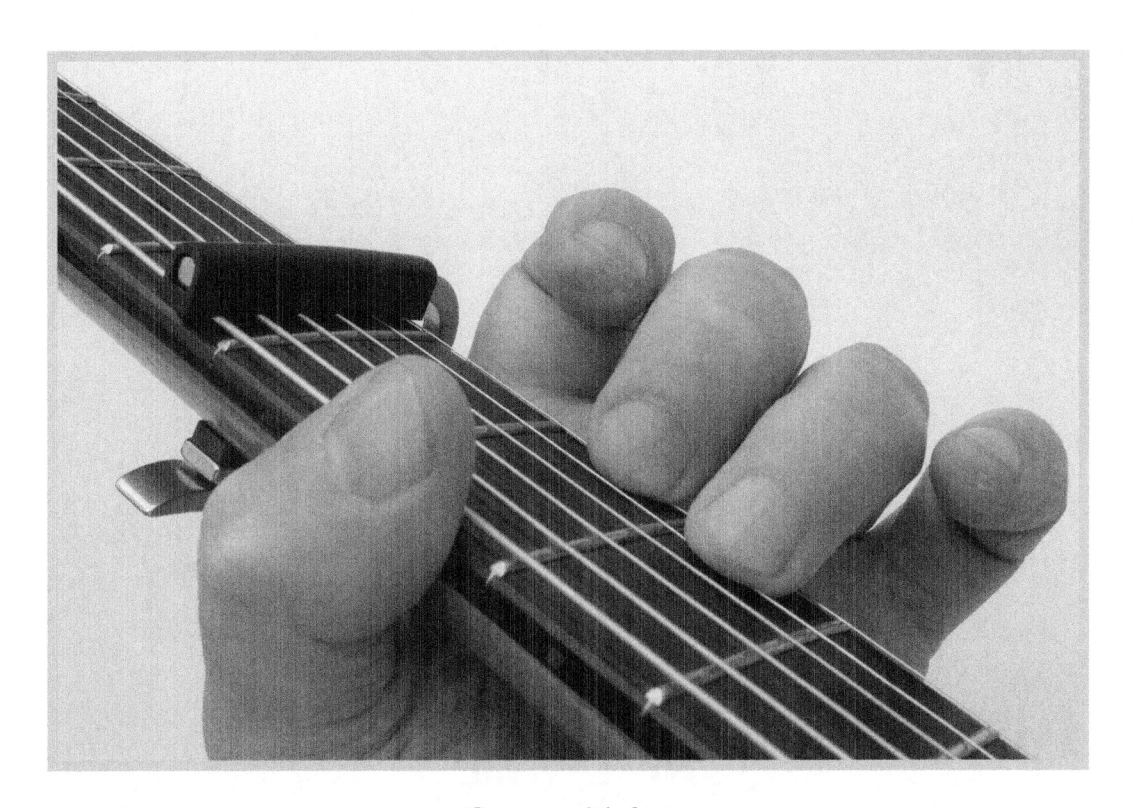

Capo on 4th fret

🎸 PLAYING EXERCISE 3

Keep repeating this chord sequence

CAPO ON 1ST FRET

G6 – Page 32

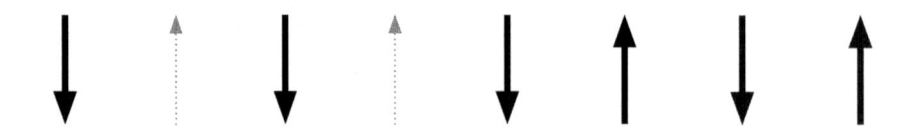

↓ ↑ ↓ ↑ ↓ ↑ ↓ ↑

G6

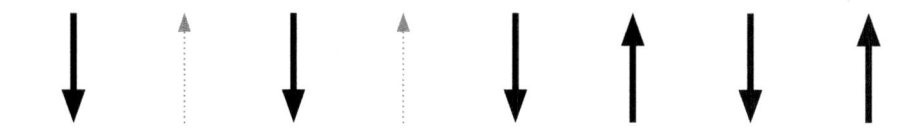

↓ ↑ ↓ ↑ ↓ ↑ ↓ ↑

CMAJ7 – Page 32

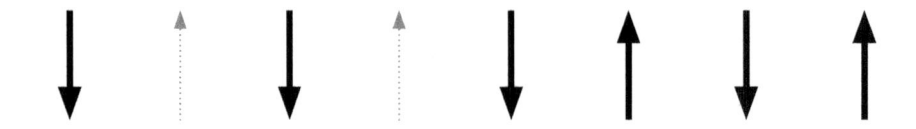

↓ ↑ ↓ ↑ ↓ ↑ ↓ ↑

CMAJ7

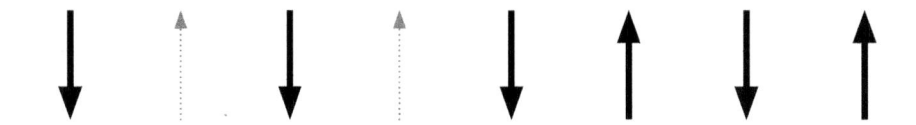

↓ ↑ ↓ ↑ ↓ ↑ ↓ ↑

🎸 SONG EXAMPLE

Waiting In Vain - Bob Marley

LESSON 6 | 63

G EASY

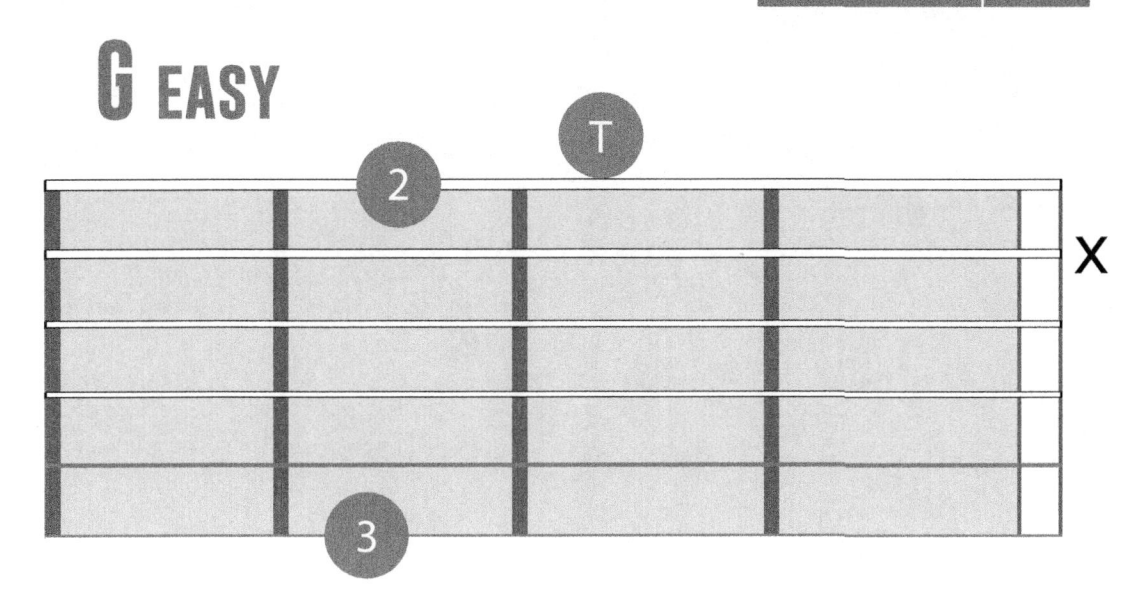

- Thumb can touch 6th string
- 5th string muted by inside of 2nd finger
- Strum 6 strings - Only 5 sound

Asus2

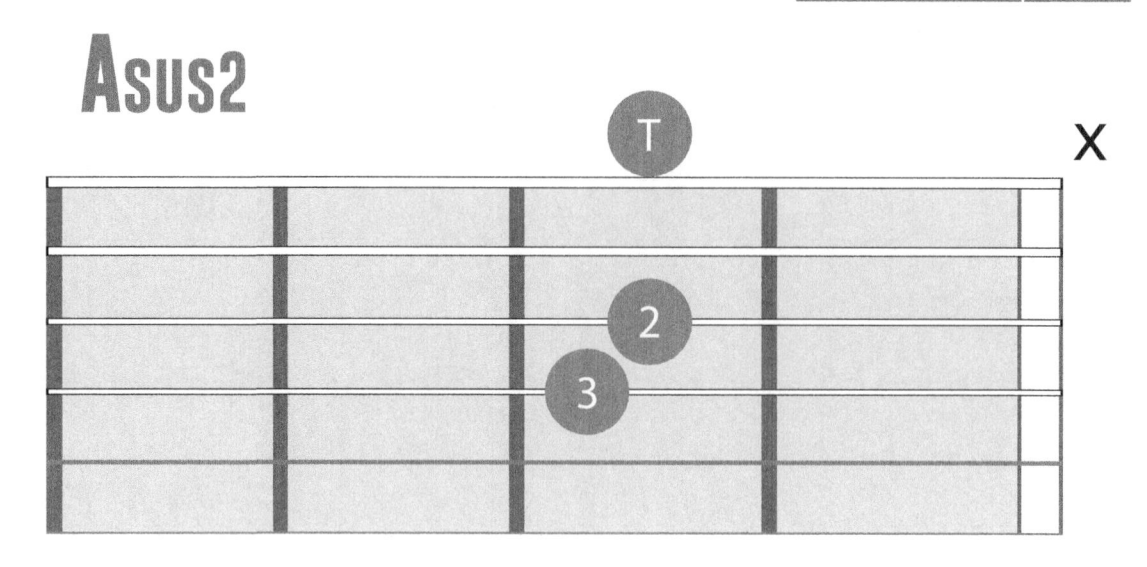

LESSON 6 | 64

- Thumb touching 6th string
- 3rd finger in corner of fret
- Strum 6 strings - Only 5 sound

LESSON 6

🎸 PLAYING EXERCISE 4

Keep repeating this chord sequence

Em - Page 32

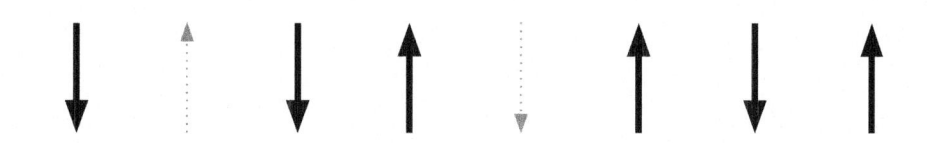

↓ ↑ ↓ ↑ ↑ ↑ ↓ ↑

G - Page 63

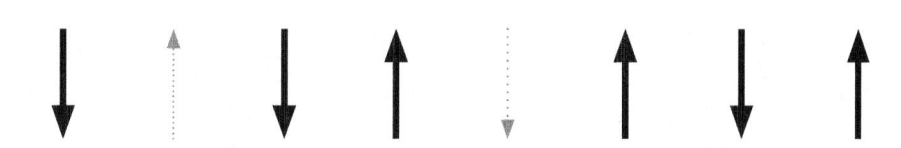

↓ ↑ ↓ ↑ ↑ ↑ ↓ ↑

D - Page 84

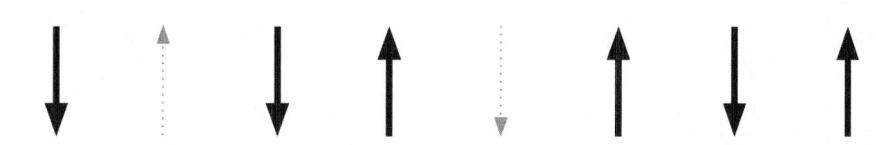

↓ ↑ ↓ ↑ ↑ ↑ ↓ ↑

Asus2 - Page 64

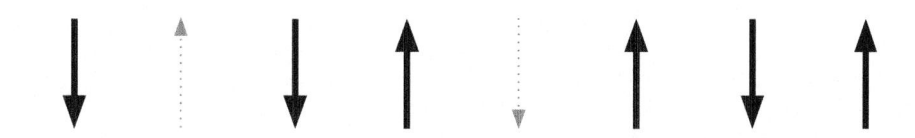

↓ ↑ ↓ ↑ ↑ ↑ ↓ ↑

🎸 SONG EXAMPLE

Mad World - Tears For Fears

PRACTICE PROGRAM
LESSON 06

- FINGER EXERCISE - **57**
- CHORD CHANGING - **51**
- GUITAR RHYTHMS - **44-45**
- PLAYING EXERCISES - **62-65**

LESSON 07

- MORE EASY CHORD CHANGES
- 3 NEW CHORDS
- 2 PLAYING EXERCISES

LESSON 7

MORE EASY CHORD CHANGES

As you saw earlier, it dramatically increases your speed of progress to learn at least two chords at a time.

The real art of your chord hand is not the chords you play. It's what happens between them.

For the next 3 chords your first finger stays in the same position. Am to D7 to Fmaj7. Again, there is no need to move it when changing from chord to chord.

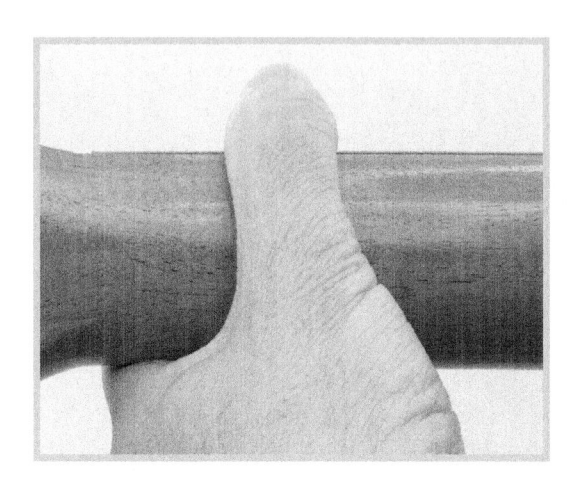

Next 3 chords - Thumb on top

LESSON 7 | 69

Am

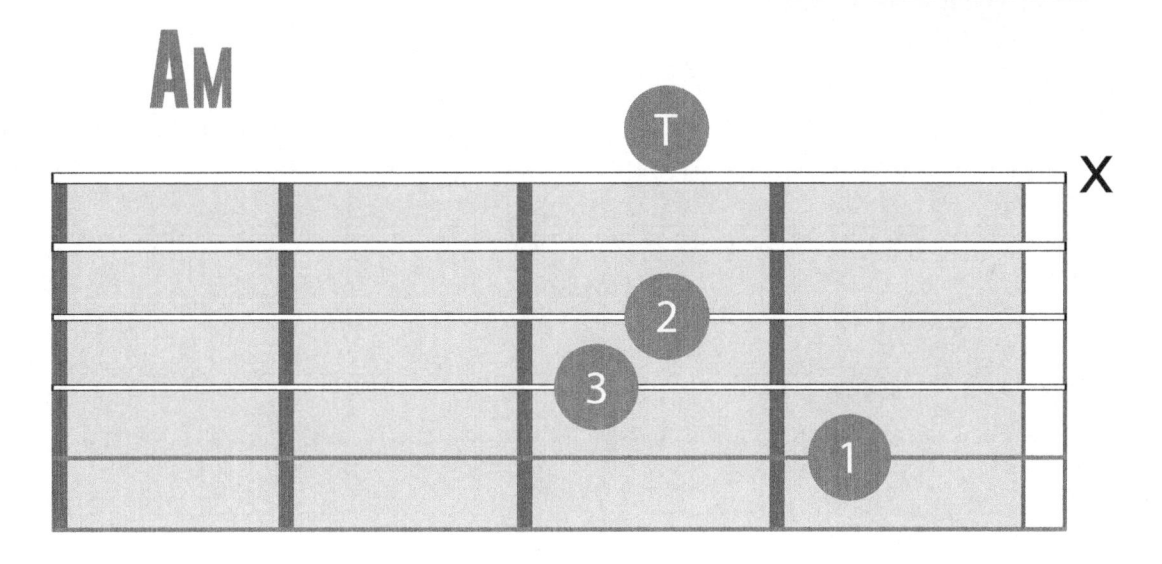

- Thumb touching 6th string
- 1st finger in corner of fret
- Strum 6 strings - Only 5 sound

LESSON 7 | 70

D7

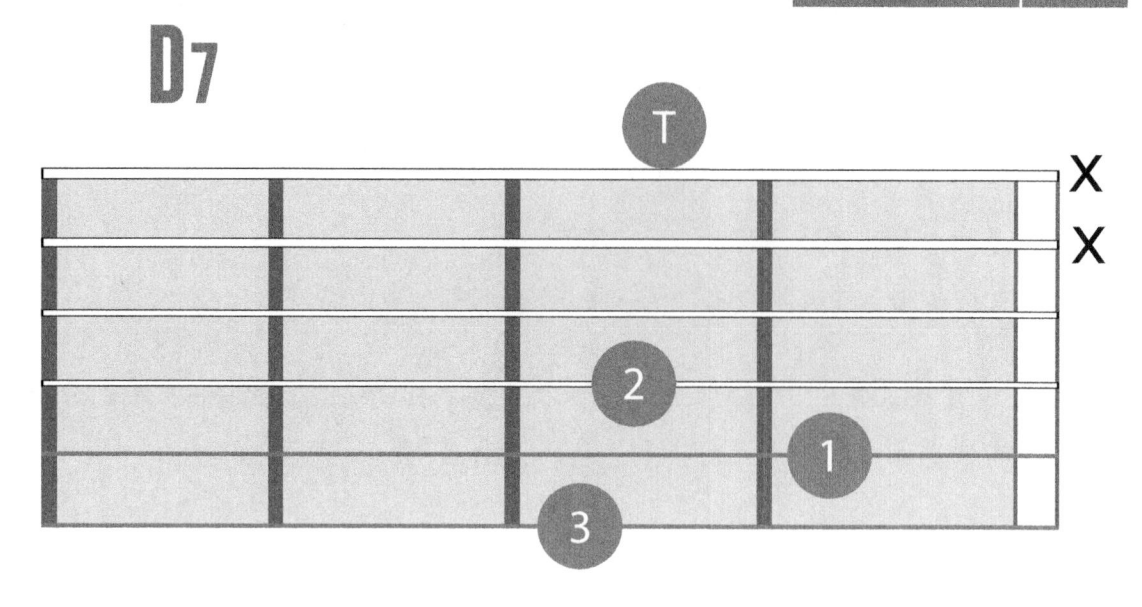

- Thumb touching 6th string
- 1st finger in corner of fret
- Strum bottom 4 strings

FMAJ7

- Thumb touching 6th string
- 1st finger in corner of fret
- Strum bottom 4 strings

LESSON 7

🎸 PLAYING EXERCISE 5
CAPO ON 2ND FRET

Am - Page 69

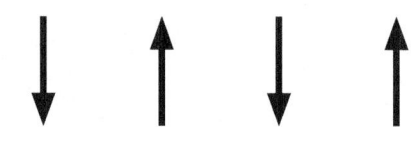

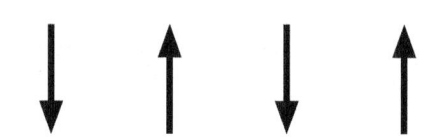

↓   ↓   ↓   ↑   ↓   ↑

D7 - Page 70

↓   ↓   ↓   ↑   ↓   ↑

Fmaj7 - Page 71

↓   ↓   ↓   ↑   ↓   ↑

Em - Page 48

↓   ↓   ↓   ↑   ↓   ↑

🎸 PLAYING TIPS

Am to D7 to Fmaj7 - Don't move 1st finger

Em - Raise your thumb

🎸 SONG EXAMPLE

Jammin - Bob Marley

LESSON 7

🎸 PLAYING EXERCISE 6

Keep repeating this chord sequence

CAPO ON 2ND FRET

Am - Page 69

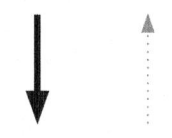

↓ ↑ ↓ ↑ ↓ ↑ ↓ ↑

G - Page 87

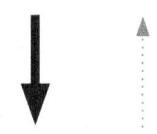

↓ ↑ ↓ ↑ ↓ ↑ ↓ ↑

D - Page 84

↓ ↑ ↓ ↑ ↓ ↑ ↓ ↑

D

↓ ↑ ↓ ↑ ↓ ↑ ↓ ↑

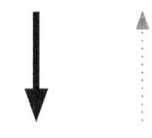

🎸 SONG EXAMPLE

Wicked Game - Chris Isaak

PRACTICE PROGRAM
LESSON 07

- FINGER EXERCISE - **57**

- PLAYING EXERCISE - **65**

- CHORD CHANGING - **69-71**

- PLAYING EXERCISES - **72-73**

LESSON 08

- HOW TO TIME GUITAR RHYTHMS
- 4 NEW CHORDS
- MORE EASY CHORD CHANGES

HOW TO TIME GUITAR RHYTHMS

1. Can you listen to a slow song that you know well?

2. As it's playing pick up your guitar and mute the strings with your chord hand. Count   1   2   3   4
3.   --   1   2   3   4.

4. If that does not work put on another slow song until you can clearly hear 1   2   3   4   --   1   2   3   4.

5. Start softly strumming the strings up and down until you are on time with the song.

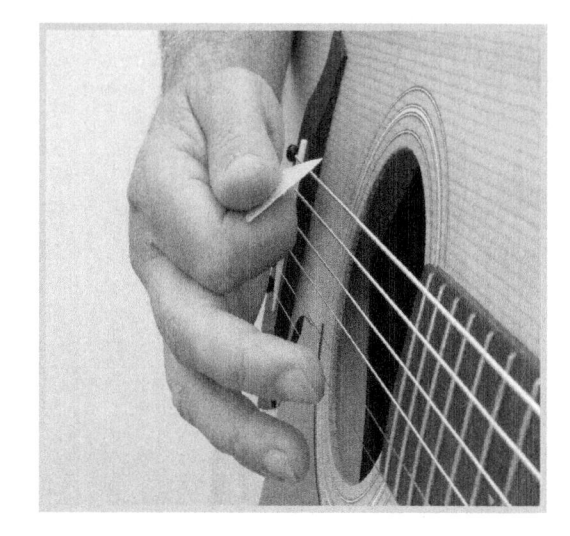

Very Important - A good hold

LESSON 8 | 77

Your chord hand keeps the strings muted while you are doing this. It's so much easier to strum when you don't have the added pressure of playing chords at the same time.

Eventually you should be able to find a rhythm to suit any song you want to play. It may not be exactly as recorded but the timing will be right. Also your own style will be starting to develop.

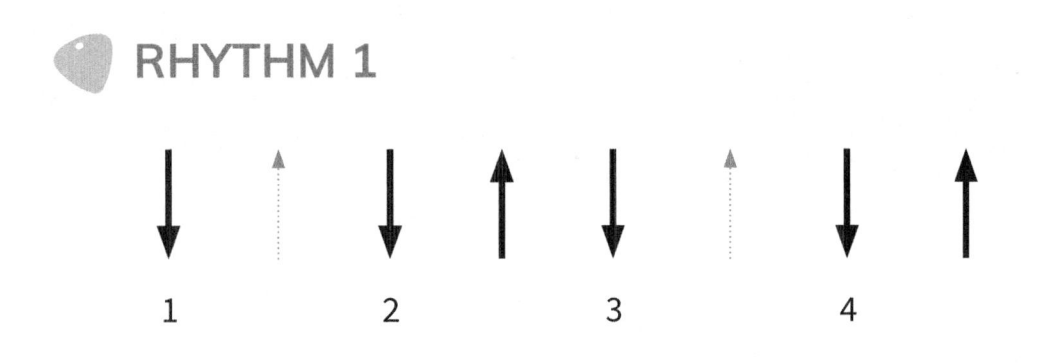

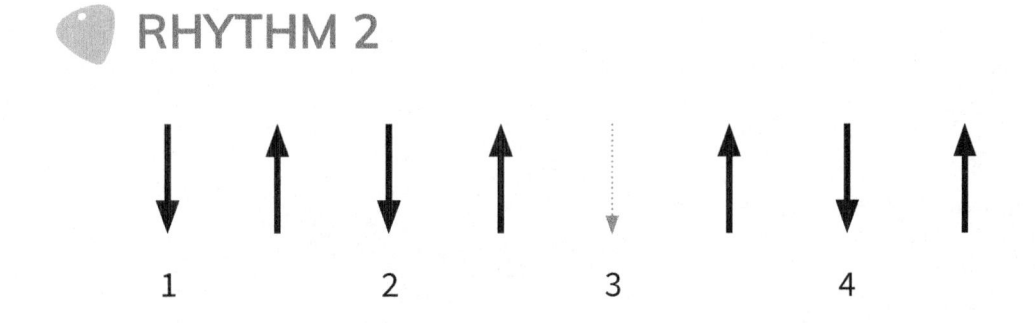

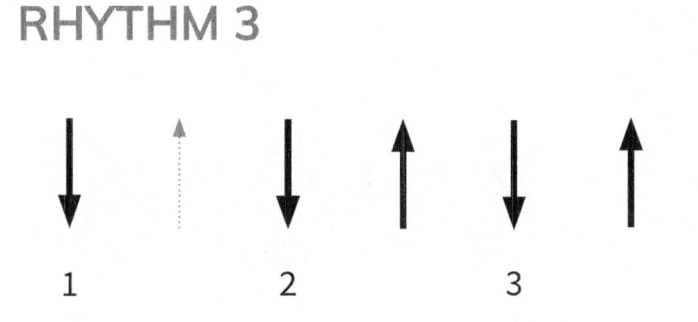

RHYTHM 1

↓ ↑ ↓ ↑ ↓ ↑ ↓ ↑
1   2   3   4

RHYTHM 2

↓ ↑ ↓ ↑ ↑ ↑ ↓ ↑
1   2   3   4

RHYTHM 3

↓ ↑ ↓ ↑ ↓ ↑
1   2   3

LESSON 8 | 78

C

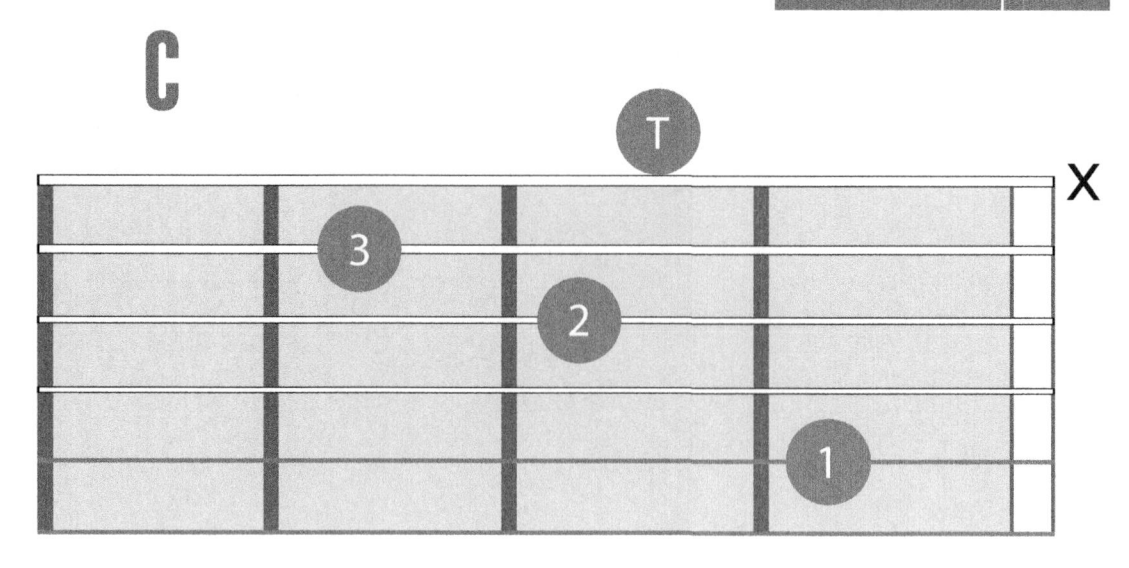

- Thumb touching 6th string
- 1st finger in corner of fret
- Strum 6 strings - Only 5 sound

A

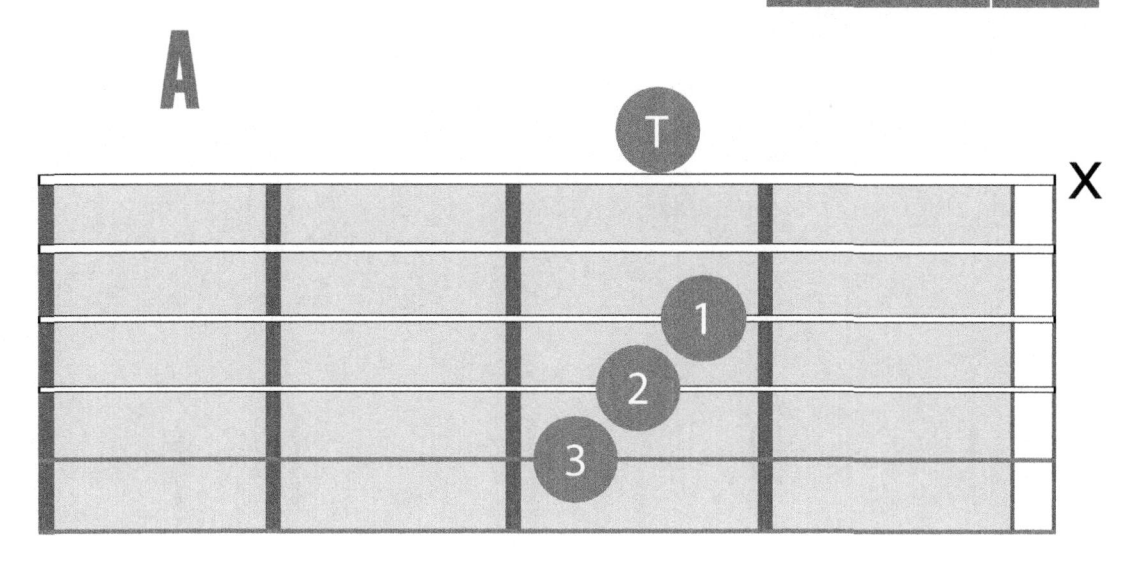

- Thumb touches 6th string
- Squeeze 3 fingers together
- Strum 6 strings - Only 5 sound

PLAYING EXERCISE 7

Keep repeating this chord sequence

CAPO ON 2ND FRET

G - Page 63

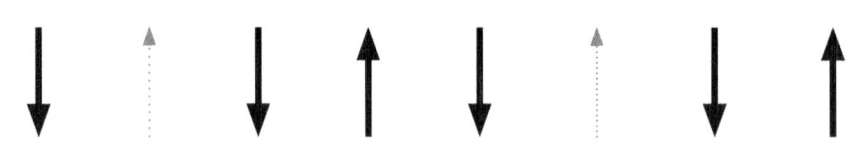

↓ ↑ ↓ ↑ ↓ ↑ ↓ ↑

G

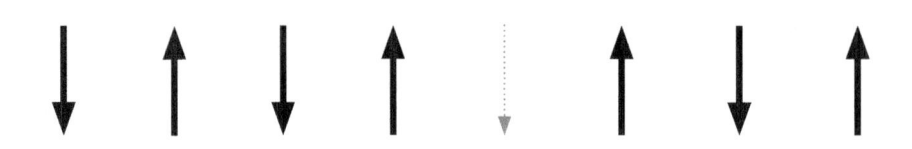

↓ ↑ ↓ ↑ ↓ ↑ ↓ ↑

Am - Page 69

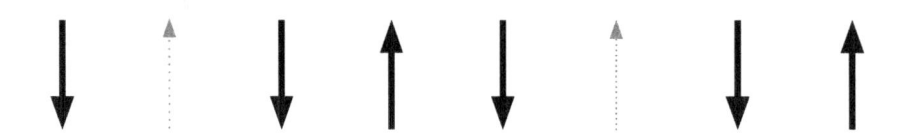

↓ ↑ ↓ ↑ ↓ ↑ ↓ ↑

Am

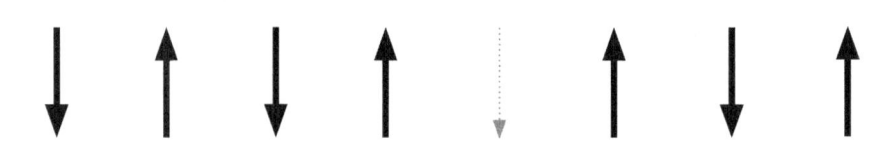

↓ ↑ ↓ ↑ ↓ ↑ ↓ ↑

LESSON 8

C - Page 78

↓ ↑ ↓ ↑ ↓ ↑ ↓ ↑

C

↓ ↑ ↓ ↑ ↑ ↓ ↓ ↑

G

↓ ↑ ↓ ↑ ↓ ↑ ↓ ↑

G

↓ ↑ ↓ ↑ ↑ ↑ ↓ ↑

🎸 PLAYING TIP

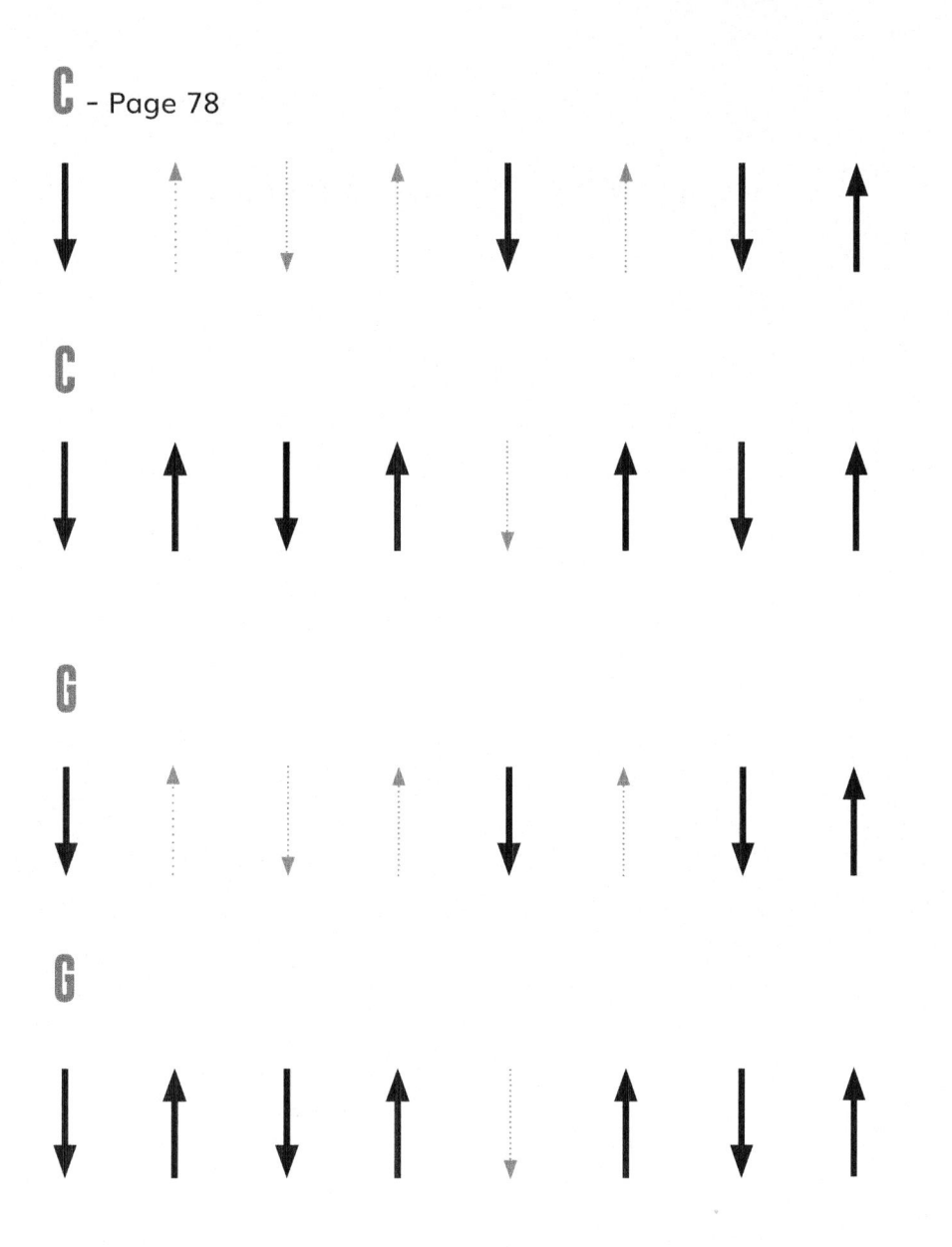

Am to C - Don't move 1st or 2nd finger

🎸 SONG EXAMPLE

What's Up - 4 Non Blondes

PLAYING EXERCISE 8

Keep repeating this chord sequence

C - Page 78

C

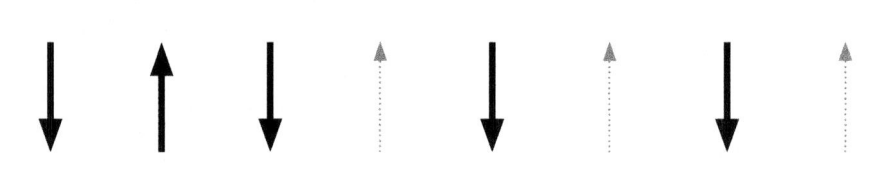

Am - Page 69

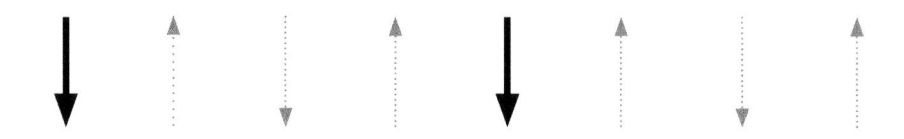

Am

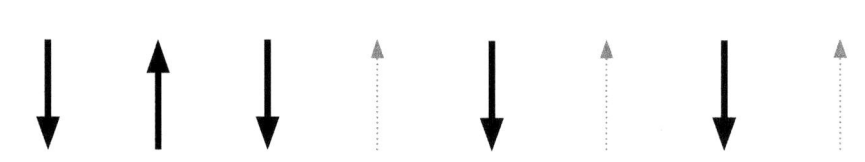

LESSON 8 | 83

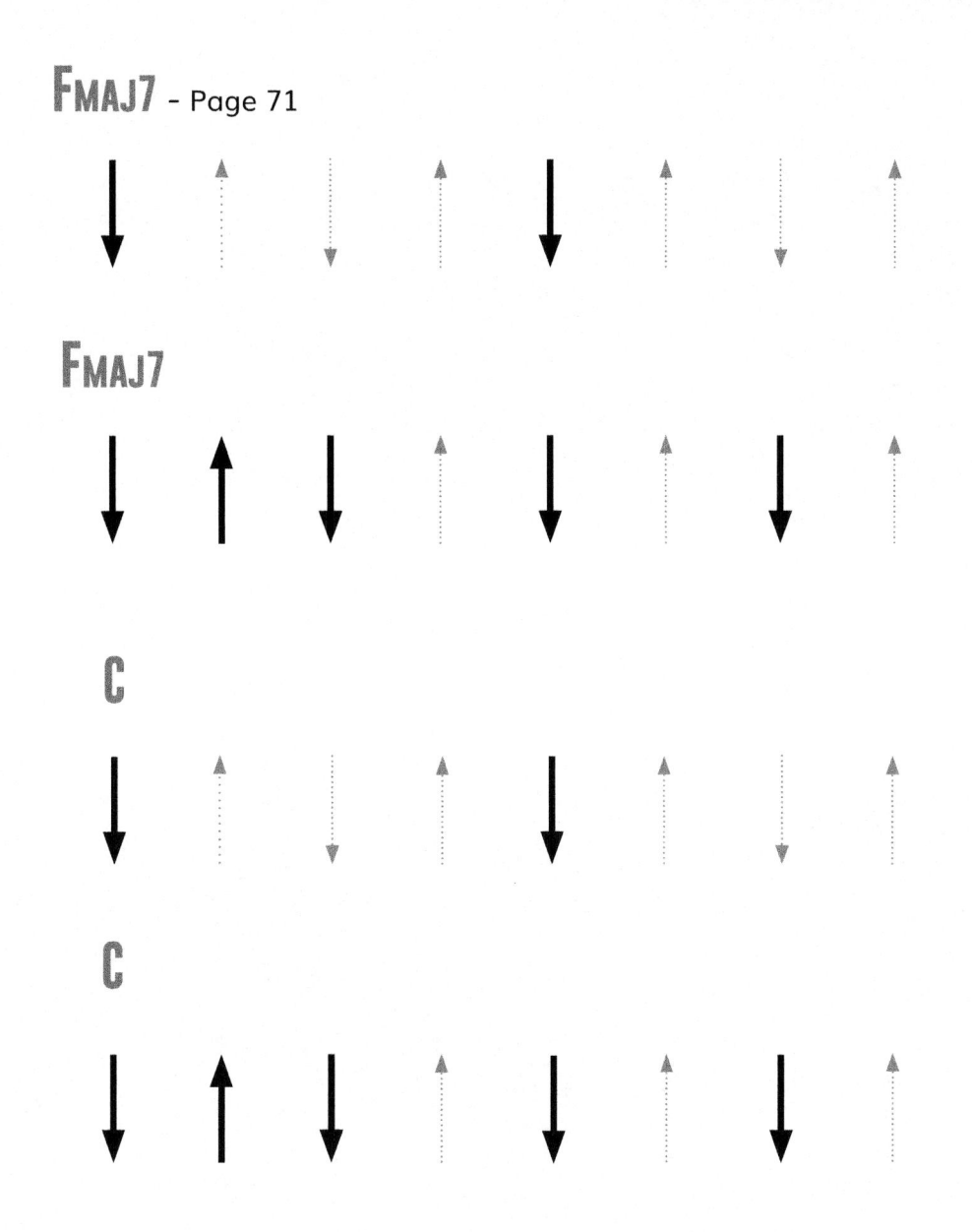

FMAJ7 - Page 71

FMAJ7

C

C

🎸 PLAYING TIP

C to Am to Fmaj7

Don't move 1st finger

🎸 SONG EXAMPLE

One - U2

LESSON 8 | 84

D

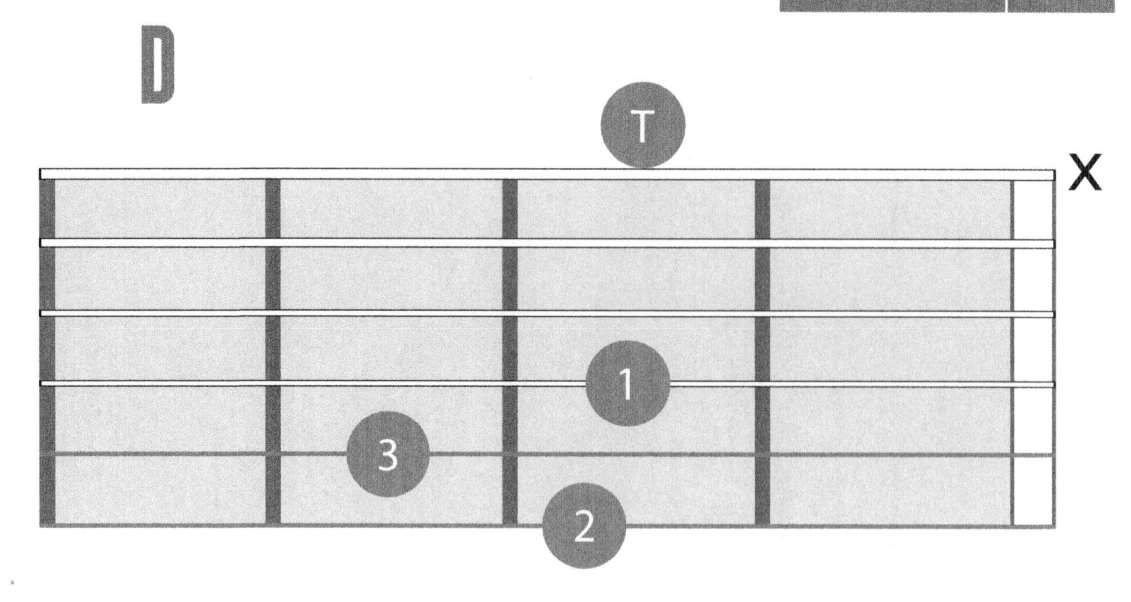

- Thumb touching 6th string
- 3rd finger in middle of fret
- Strum 6 strings - Only 5 sound

A7sus4

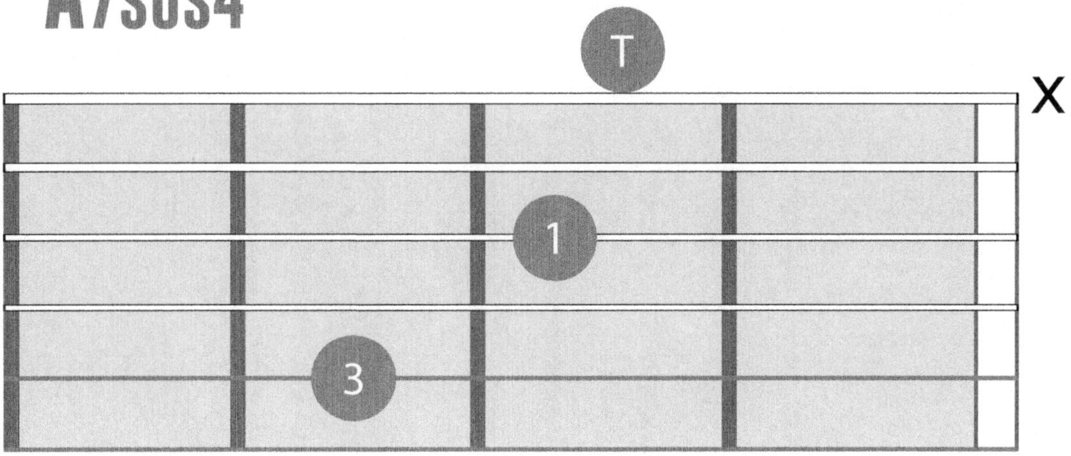

- Thumb touching 6th string
- 3rd finger in middle of fret
- Strum 6 strings - Only 5 sound

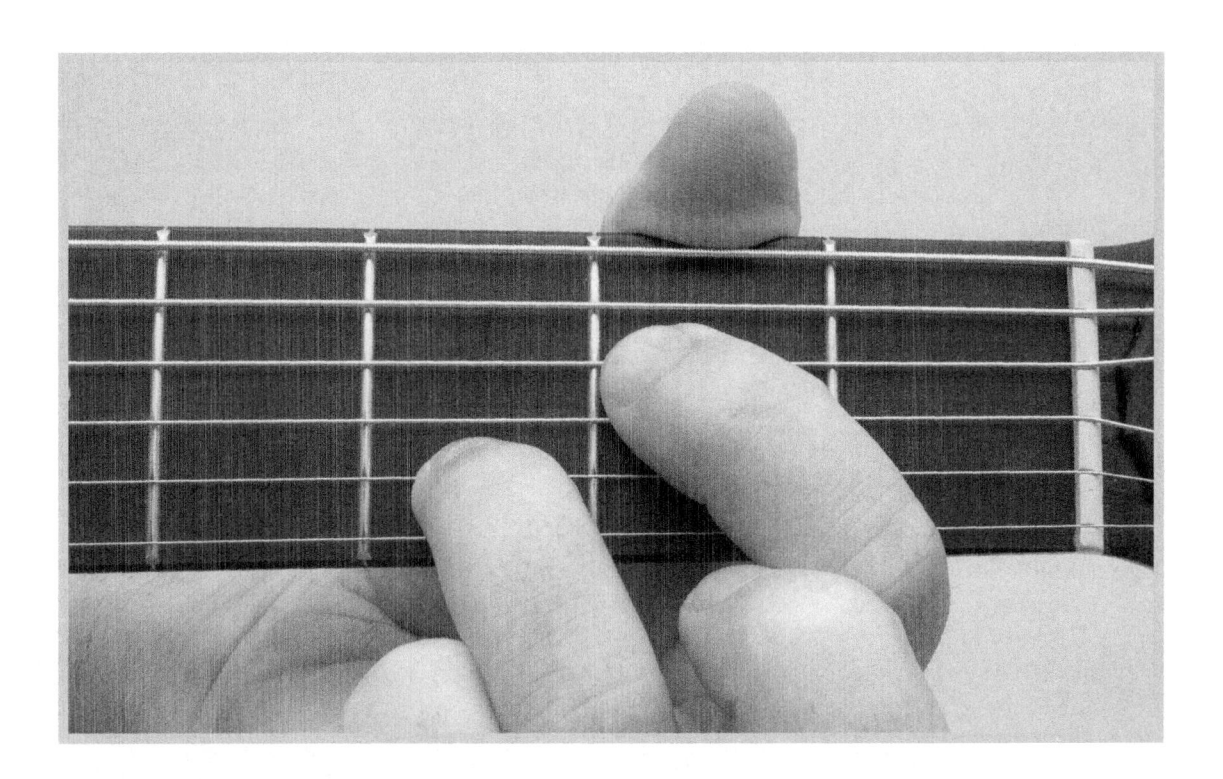

CADD9

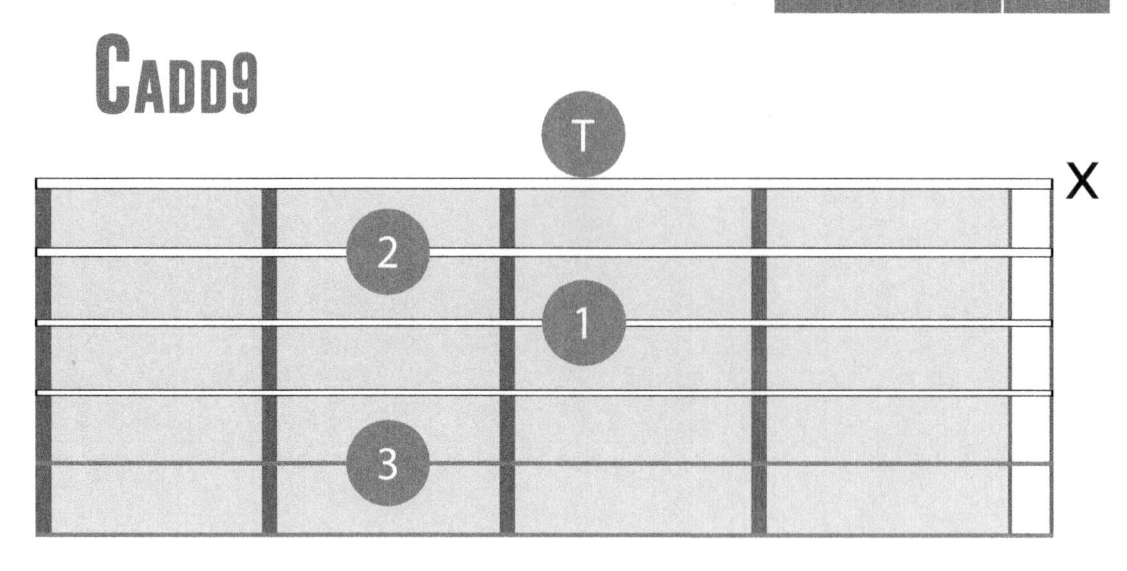

- Thumb touching 6th string
- 3rd finger in middle of fret
- Strum 6 strings - Only 5 sound

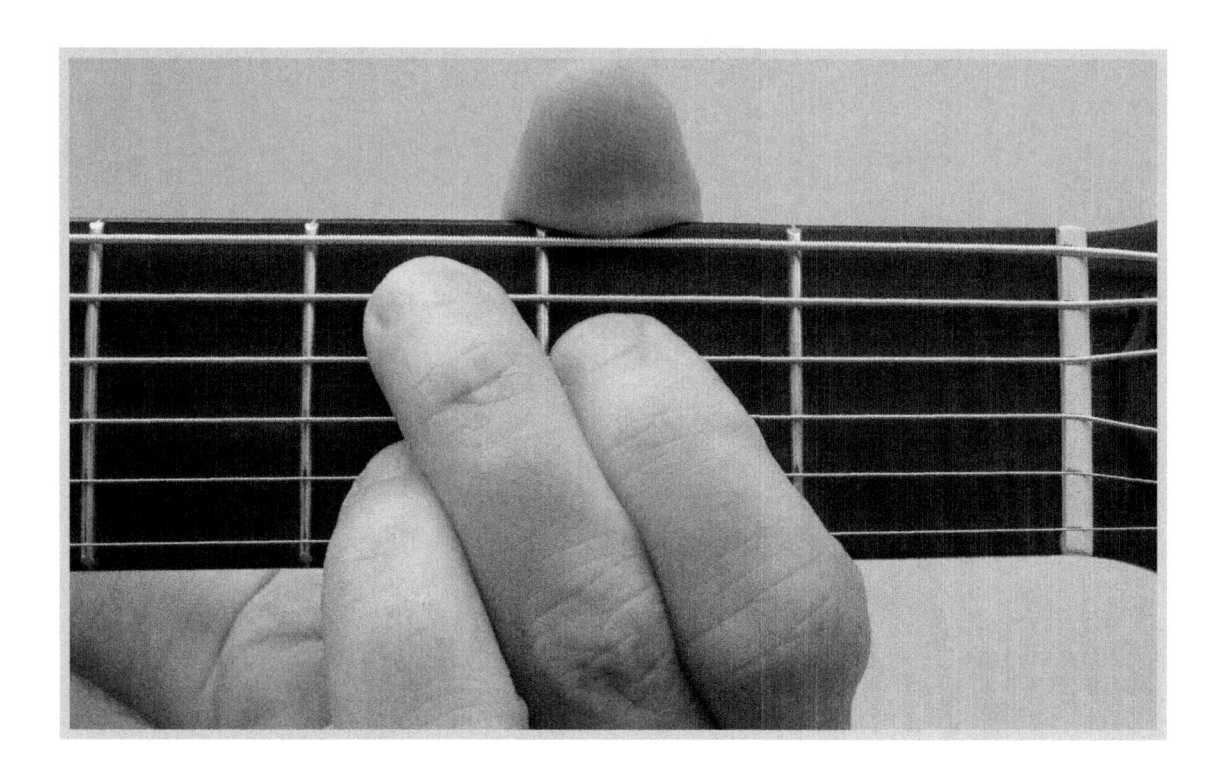

LESSON 8 | 86

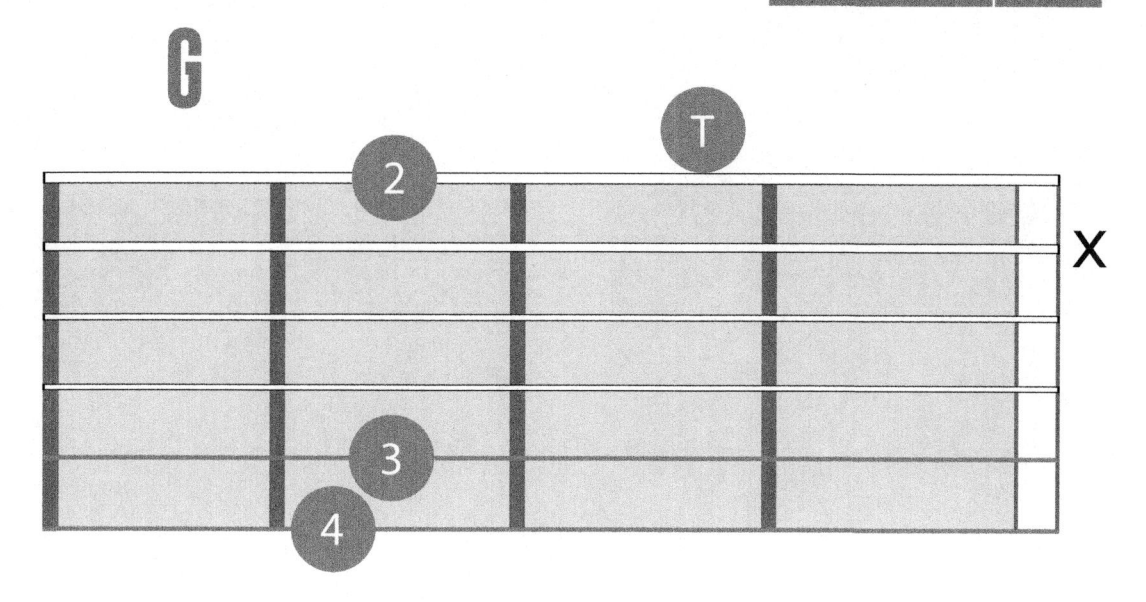

G

- Thumb may or may not touch 6th string
- 5th string muted by inside of 2nd finger
- Strum 6 strings - Only 5 sound

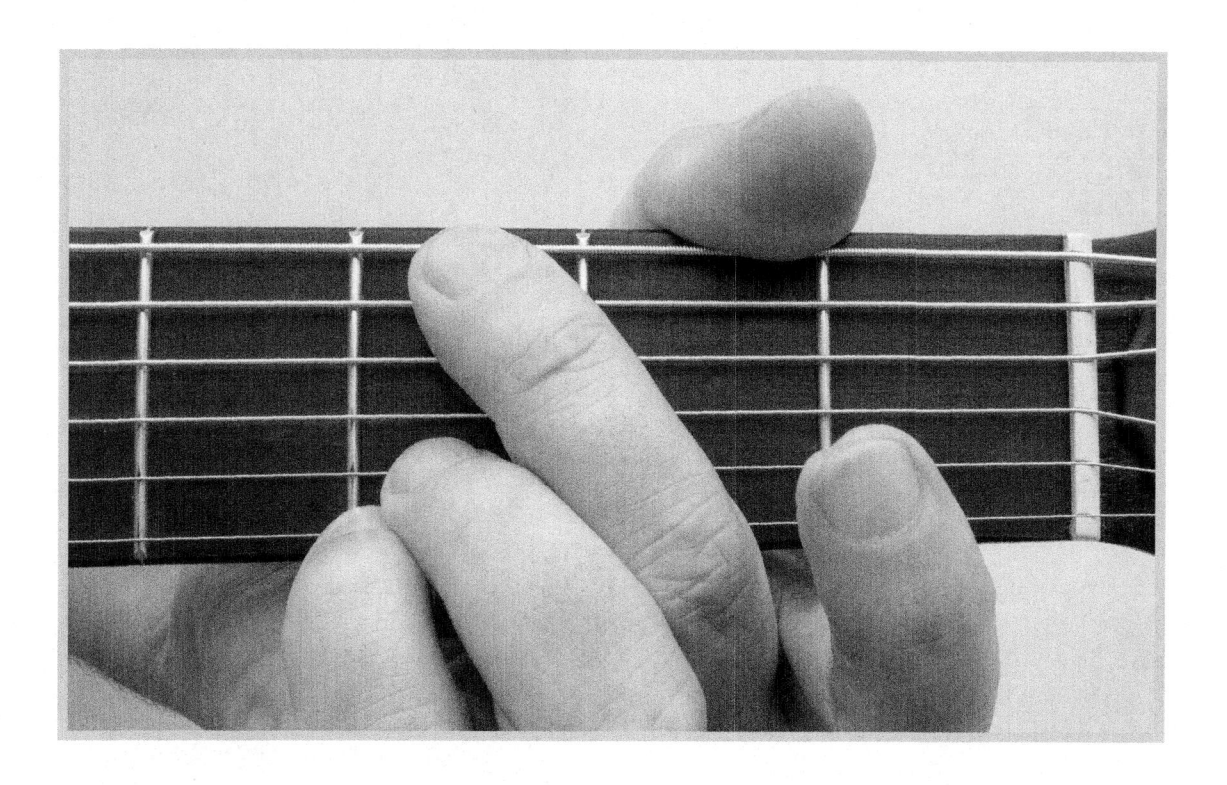

88   LESSON 8

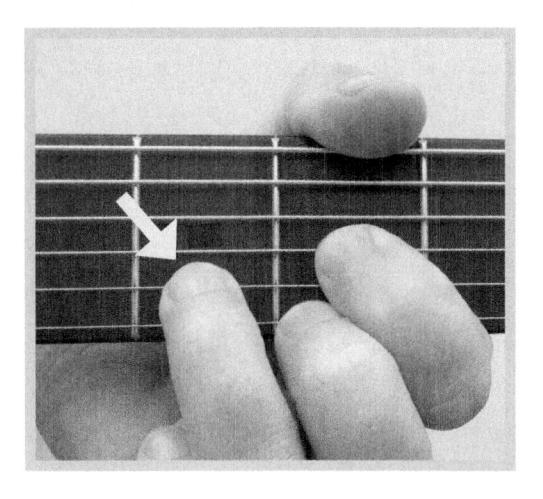

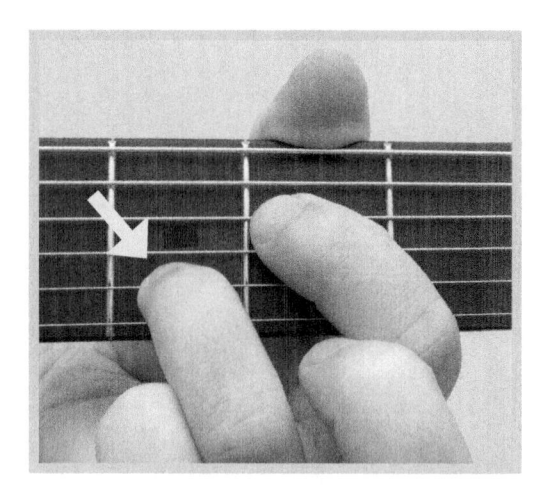

🎸 PLAYING TIPS

You can play tens of thousands of songs on guitar without moving your thumb, 3rd finger, or triangle.

This keeps your fingers close to the strings and your chord changing becomes much faster.

If you look closely at all these chords you'll see:

1. The 3rd finger is in the same place for all of them

2. The 3rd finger stays constantly pressed into the string

3. The Guitar Triangle

4. The 1st and 2nd fingers do most of the changing. Your hand stays almost still.

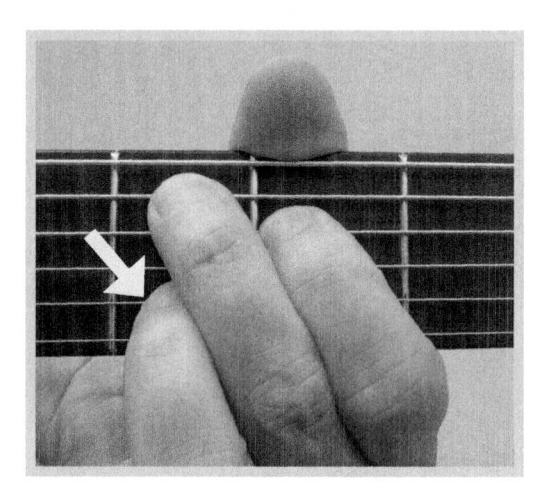

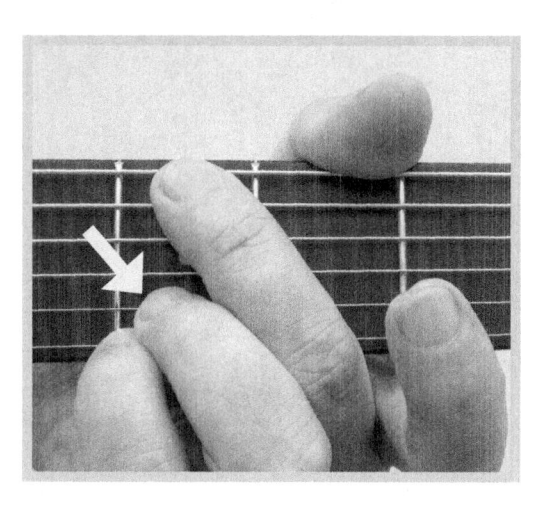

LESSON 8 | 89

🎸 PLAYING EXERCISE 9

Keep repeating this chord sequence

CAPO ON 3RD FRET

D - Page 84   **G** - Page 87

↓   ↓   Let G chord sound

G   **D**   **A7sus4** - Page 85

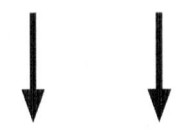

↓   ↓   ↓   Let A7sus4 chord sound

🎸 PLAYING TIP

When changing, don't move your

1. Thumb
2. 3rd finger
3. Triangle

🎸 SONG EXAMPLE

Free Falling - Tom Petty

PRACTICE PROGRAM
LESSON 08

- FINGER EXERCISE - **57**
- GUITAR RHYTHMS - **44-45**
- PLAYING TIPS - **88**
- PLAYING EXERCISES - **80-83**

LESSON 09

- 2 NEW CHORDS
- 4 POPULAR CHORD SEQUENCES
- HOW TO READ GUITAR TABLATURE

LESSON 9 | 92

Asus4

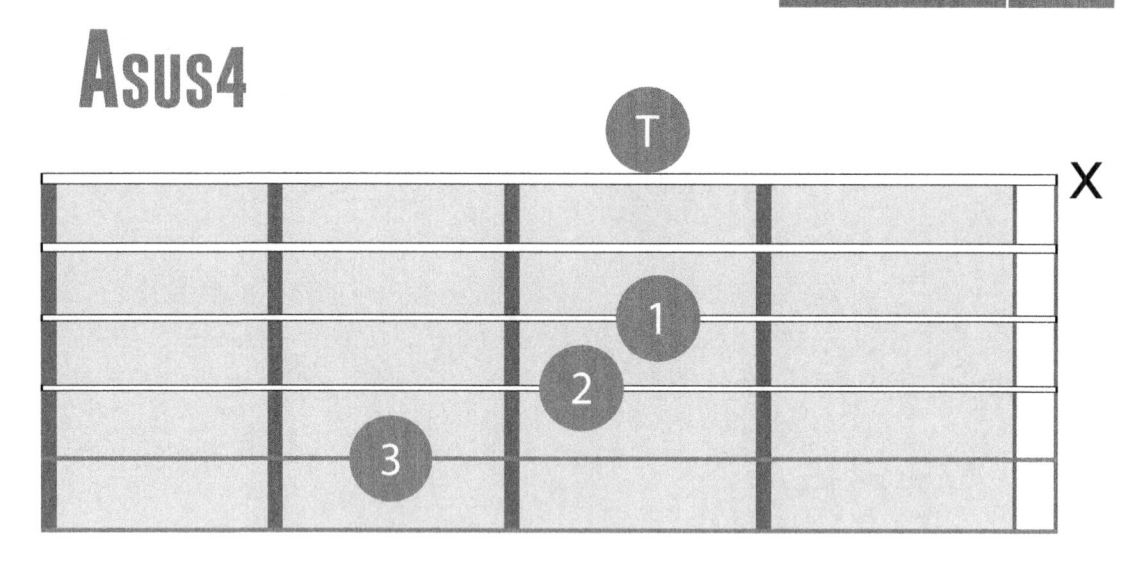

- Thumb touching 6th string
- 3rd finger in middle of fret
- Strum 6 strings - Only 5 sound

A_M7

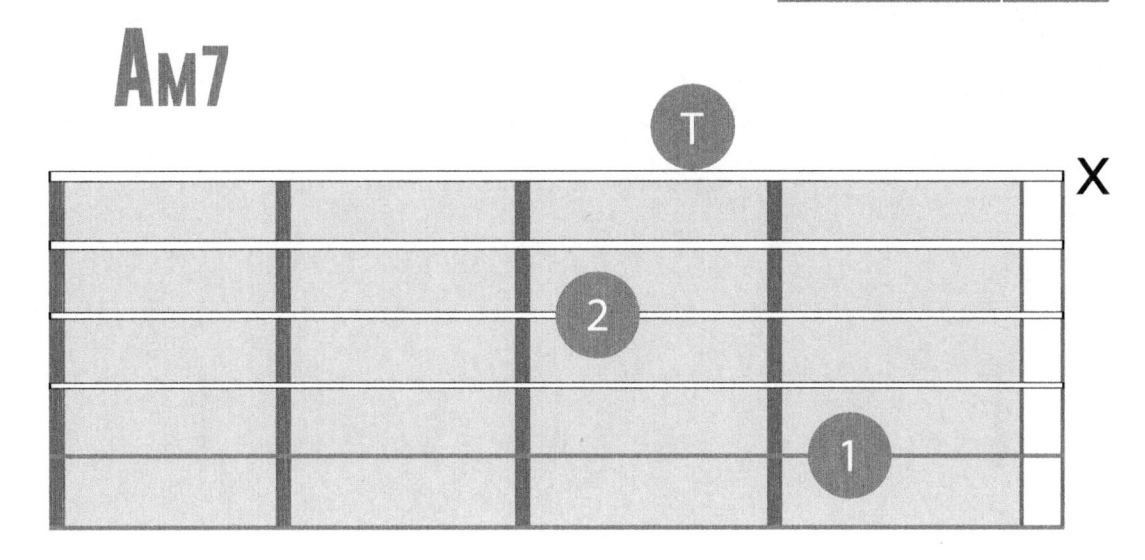

- Thumb touching 6th string
- 1st finger in corner of fret
- Strum 6 strings - Only 5 sound

PLAYING EXERCISE 10

Keep repeating this chord sequence

PLAY FAST

D - Page 84

↓ ↑ ↓ ↑ ↓ ↑ ↓ ↑

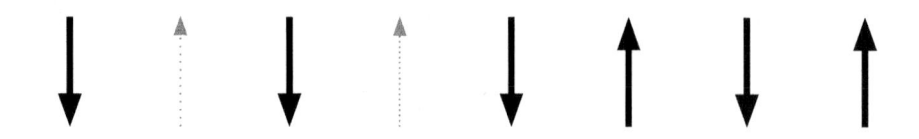

Cadd9 - Page 86

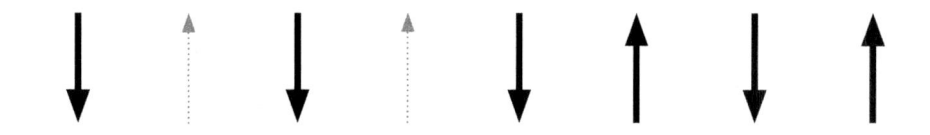

↓ ↑ ↓ ↑ ↓ ↑ ↓ ↑

G - Page 87

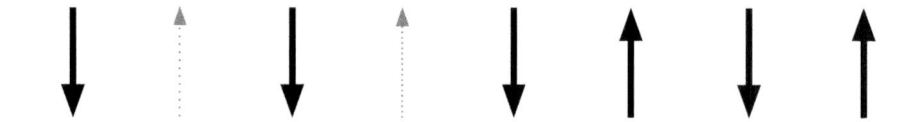

↓ ↑ ↓ ↑ ↓ ↑ ↓ ↑

G

↓ ↑ ↓ ↑ ↓ ↑ ↓ ↑

PLAYING TIP

Don't move 3rd finger

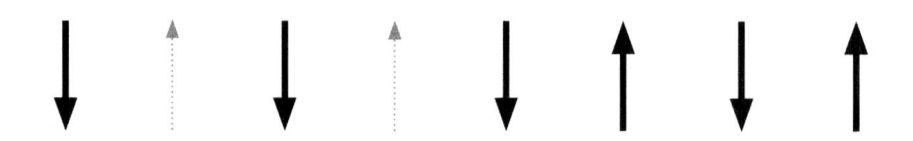

SONG EXAMPLE

Sweet Home Alabama

PLAYING EXERCISE 11

Keep repeating this chord sequence

G - Page 87

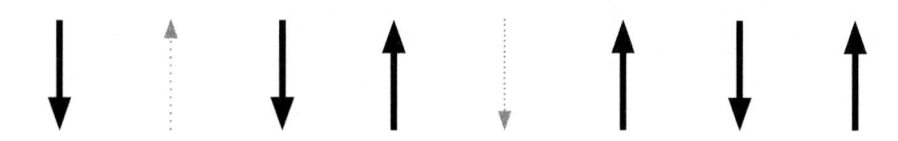

↓ ↑ ↓ ↑ ↓ ↓ ↑ ↓ ↑

D - Page 84

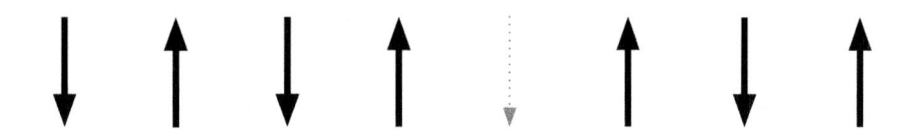

↓ ↑ ↓ ↑ ↓ ↑ ↓ ↑

CADD9 - Page 86

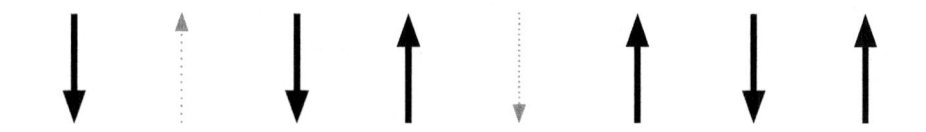

↓ ↑ ↓ ↑ ↓ ↑ ↓ ↑

CADD9

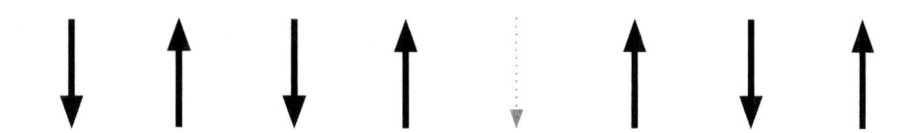

↓ ↑ ↓ ↑ ↓ ↑ ↓ ↑

SONG EXAMPLE

Knocking On Heavens Door

Bob Dylan

PLAYING EXERCISE 12

Keep repeating this chord sequence

G - Page 87

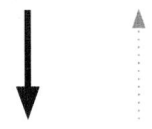

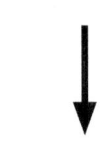

↓ ↑ ↓ ↑ ↑ ↓ ↓ ↑

Cadd9 - Page 86

↓ ↑ ↓ ↑ ↓ ↑ ↓ ↑

G

↓ ↑ ↓ ↑ ↓ ↑ ↓ ↑

Cadd9

↓ ↑ ↓ ↑ ↓ ↑ ↓ ↑

LESSON 9 | 97

G

Cadd9

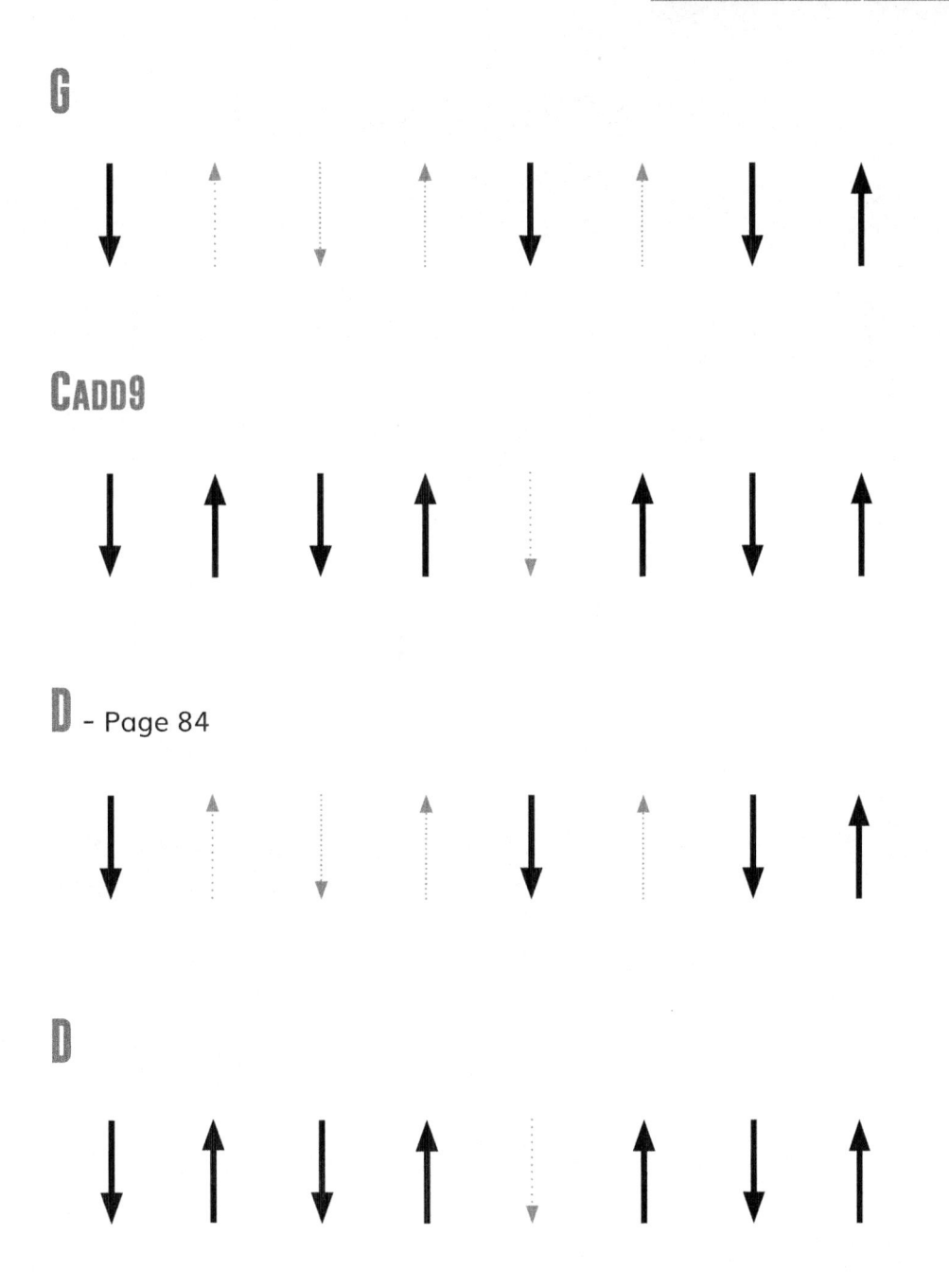

D - Page 84

D

🎸 SONG EXAMPLE

Leaving On A Jetplane - John Denver

PLAYING EXERCISE 14

Keep repeating this chord sequence

D - Page 84

↓　　↓　　↑↓↑↓　↓　↓↑

D

↓　　↓　　↑↓↑↓　↓　↓↑

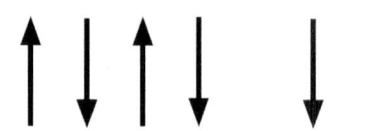

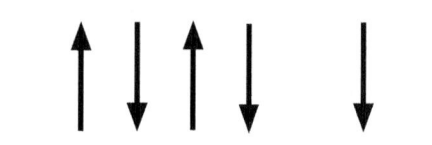

Asus4 - Page 92

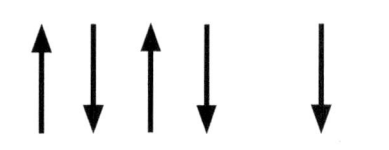

↓　　↓　　↑↓↑↓　↓　↓↑

Asus4

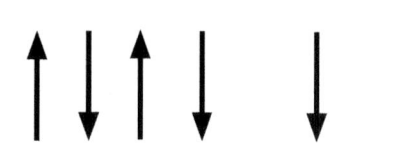

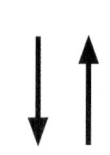

↓　　↓　　↑↓↑↓　↓　↓↑

LESSON 9

Cadd9 - Page 86

↓ ↓ ↑↓↑↓ ↓ ↓↑

Cadd9

↓ ↓ ↑↓↑↓ ↓ ↓↑

G - Page 87

↓ ↓ ↑↓↑↓ ↓ ↓↑

G

↓ ↓ ↑↓↑↓ ↓ ↓↑

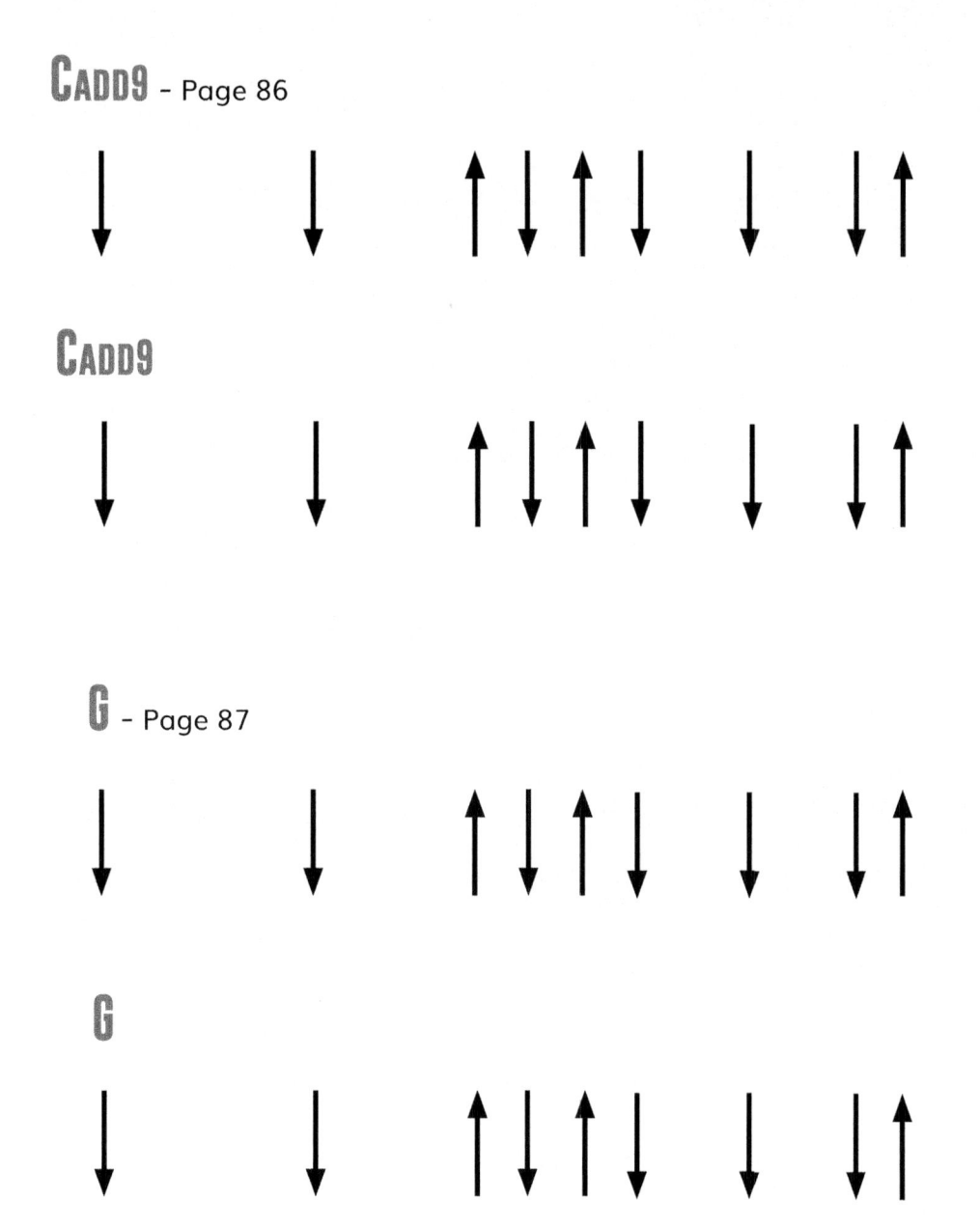

PLAYING TIP

Don't move 3rd finger

SONG EXAMPLE

Linger - The Cranberries

HOW TO READ GUITAR TABLATURE

Guitar tablature is very easy to learn. The six horizontal lines represent the six strings on the guitar. The numbers are the frets to play. 0 = Open String. 2 = 2nd Fret.

If the numbers are written one after another, you pick the strings one at a time (after you have fingered the chord). If the numbers are written on top of each other, you play all the strings at once (strumming).

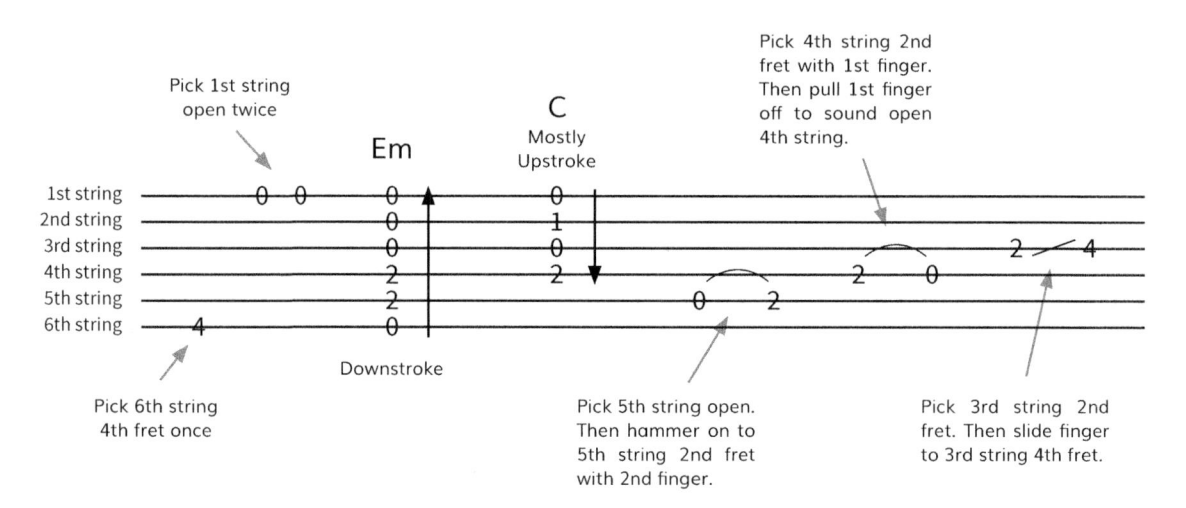

```
                    Pick 1st string                              Pick 4th string 2nd
                    open twice                                   fret with 1st finger.
                                          C                      Then pull 1st finger
                                       Mostly                    off to sound open
                             Em        Upstroke                  4th string.

1st string ─────────0──0────0─────────0─────────────────────────────────────────
2nd string ─────────────────0─────────1─────────────────────────────────────────
3rd string ─────────────────0─────────0────────────────────────────────2──4─────
4th string ─────────────────2─────────2────────────────────2──0─────────────────
5th string ─────────────────2──────────────────────0──2─────────────────────────
6th string ────4────────────0───────────────────────────────────────────────────

                   ↑                                                    
        ↑           Downstroke         ↑                ↑                ↑
   Pick 6th string                  Pick 5th string open.         Pick 3rd string 2nd
   4th fret once                    Then hammer on to              fret. Then slide finger
                                    5th string 2nd fret            to 3rd string 4th fret.
                                    with 2nd finger.
```

LESSON 9   101

PLAYING EXERCISE 15

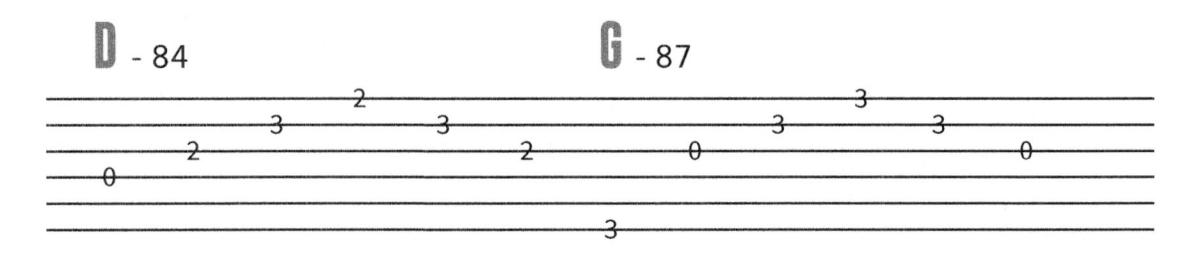

D - 84   **G** - 87

```
|----------------2----------------|--------------3--3-----|
|-------3-----3------3------------|-----3-----3-----------|
|----2-----------------2-----0----|--------0--------------|
|-0-------------------------------|-----------------------|
|---------------------------------|-----------------------|
|-----------------3---------------|-----------------------|
```

HOW TO CONVERT SHEET MUSIC INTO GUITAR TABLATURE

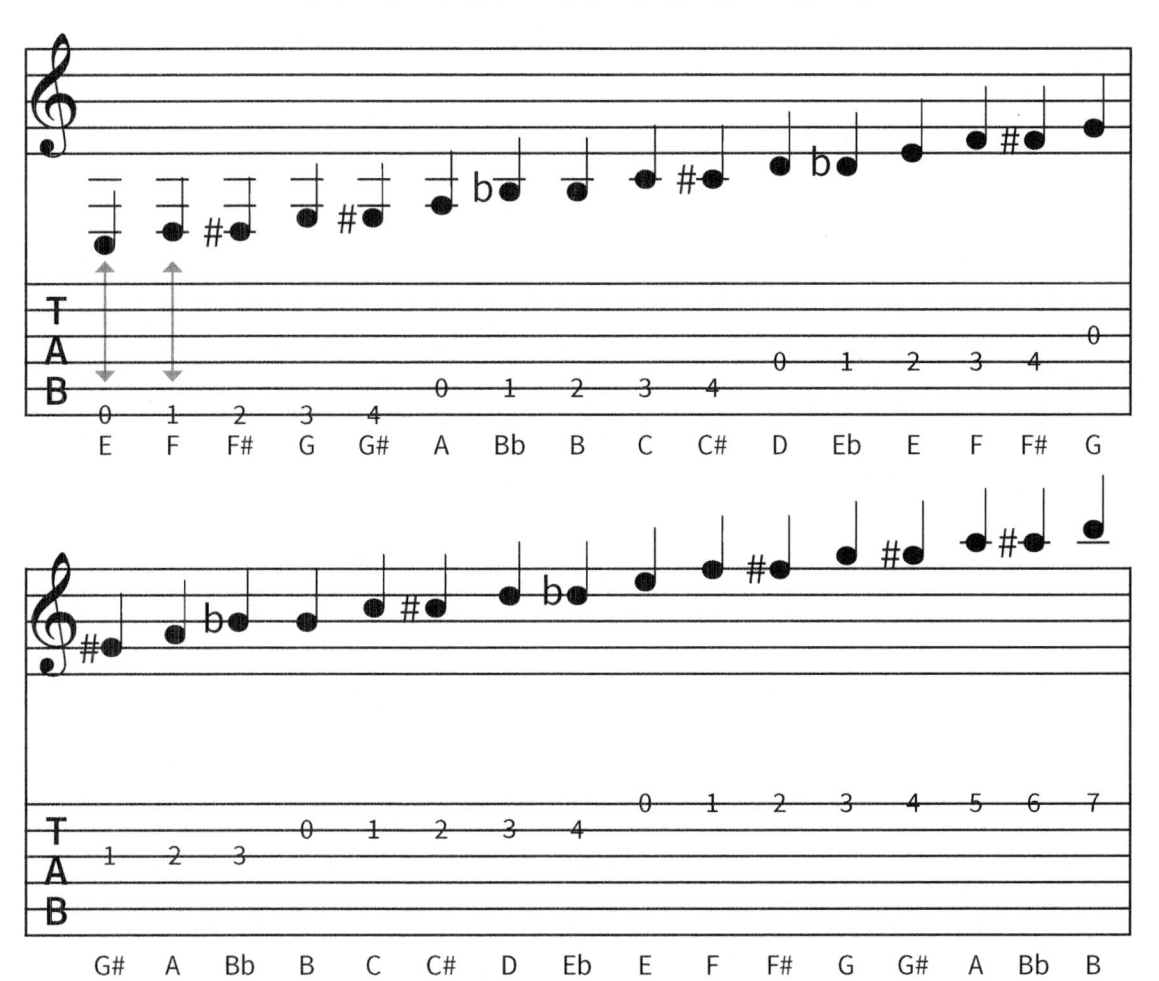

```
T |--------------------------------------------------0--|
A |--------------------------------0--1--2--3--4--------|
B |--0--1--2--3--4--0--1--2--3--4-----------------------|
   E  F  F# G  G# A  Bb B  C  C# D  Eb E  F  F# G
```

```
T |-----------------------------0--1--2--3--4--5--6--7--|
A |-----------0--1--2--3--4-----------------------------|
B |-1--2--3---------------------------------------------|
   G# A  Bb B  C  C# D  Eb E  F  F# G  G# A  Bb B
```

PRACTICE PROGRAM
LESSON 09

- FINGER EXERCISE - **57**
- PLAYING EXERCISES - **80-83**
- PLAYING TIPS - **88**
- PLAYING EXERCISES - **94-99**

LESSON 10

- HOW TO PLAY FINGERSTYLE GUITAR
- 6 POPULAR FINGERSTYLES
- 50 MOST PLAYED GUITAR CHORDS

HOW TO PLAY FINGERSTYLE GUITAR

Competent guitarists play by feel and without looking at their picking hand. They do this by playing from a reference point.

Many have the heel pad of their hand lightly resting on the bridge pins (pictured right).

Others have the 3rd or 4th finger on the guitar (Next page).

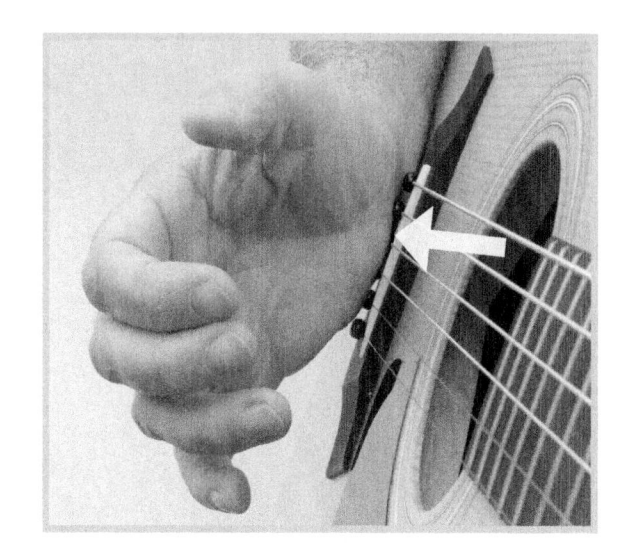

LESSON 10 | 105

HITCH HIKERS THUMB

T

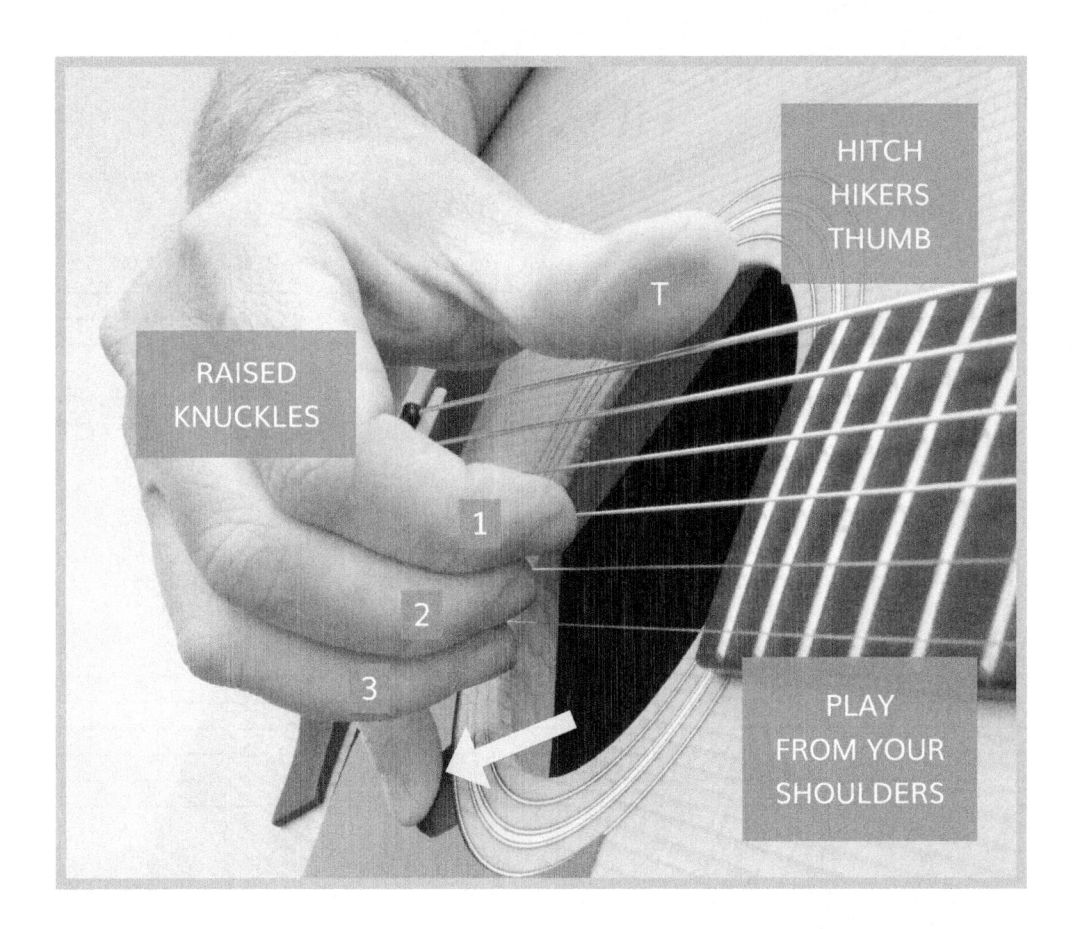

RAISED KNUCKLES

1
2
3

PLAY FROM YOUR SHOULDERS

🎸 PLAYING TIPS

- Visualize a ball in your hand
- Thumb picks down
- Fingers pick up
- Thumb picks a little louder than fingers

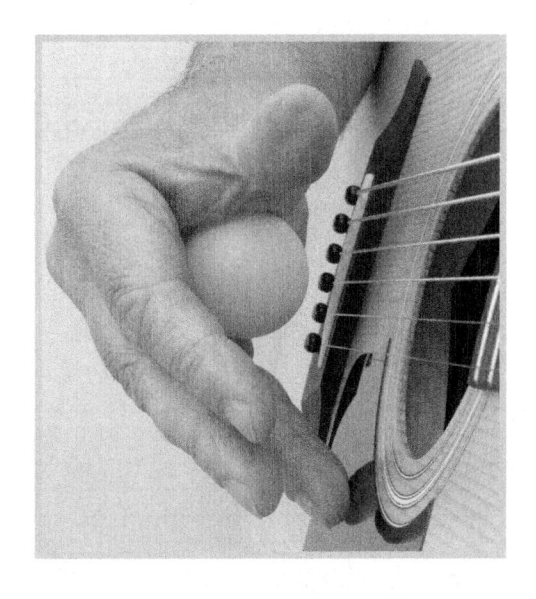

ROMANZA

Fingerstyle Guitar

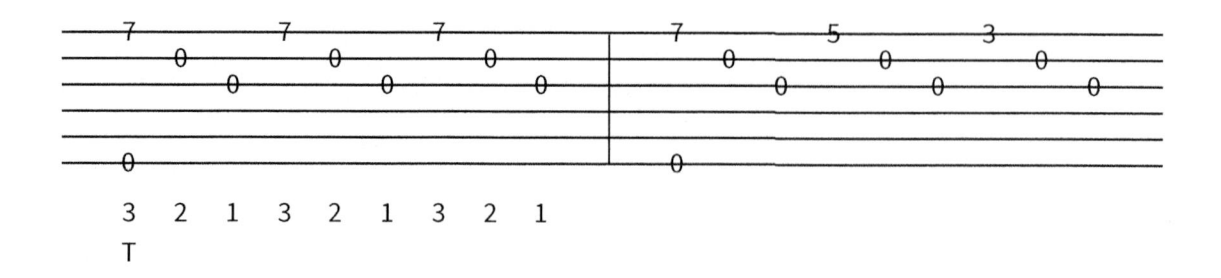

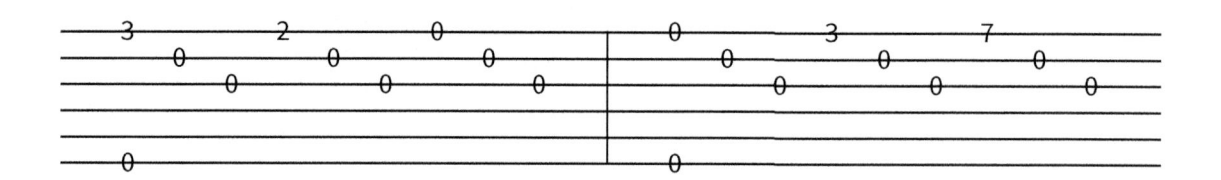

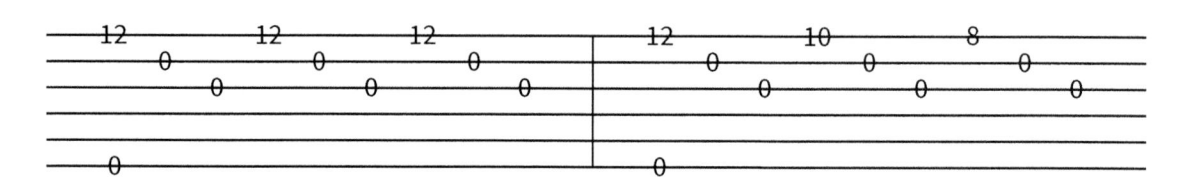

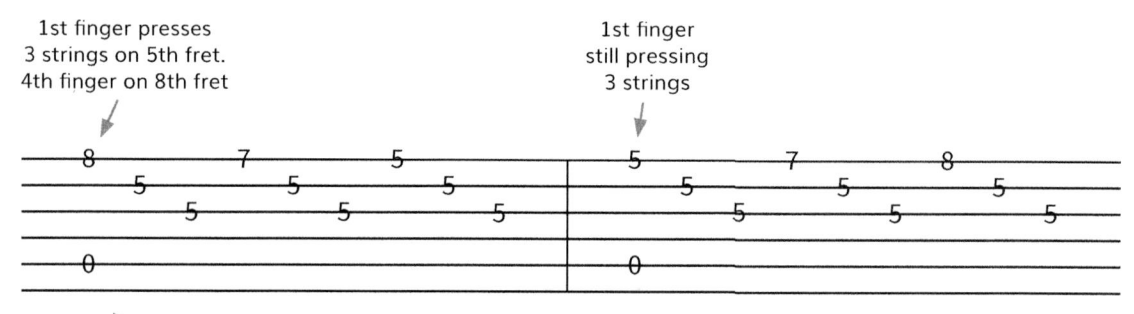

```
-----7-------7-------7--------|------7-------5-------3-------
--------0-------0-------0-----|--------0-------0-------0-----
-----------0-------0-------0--|-----------0-------0-------0--
------------------------------|------------------------------
--0---------------------------|--0---------------------------
------------------------------|------------------------------
 3   2   1   3   2   1   3   2   1
 T
```

```
-----3-------2-------0--------|------0-------3-------7-------
--------0-------0-------0-----|--------0-------0-------0-----
-----------0-------0-------0--|-----------0-------0-------0--
------------------------------|------------------------------
--0---------------------------|--0---------------------------
------------------------------|------------------------------
```

```
-----12------12------12-------|-----12------10------8--------
--------0-------0-------0-----|--------0-------0-------0-----
-----------0-------0-------0--|-----------0-------0-------0--
------------------------------|------------------------------
--0---------------------------|--0---------------------------
------------------------------|------------------------------
```

1st finger presses
3 strings on 5th fret.
4th finger on 8th fret

1st finger
still pressing
3 strings

```
-----8-------7-------5--------|------5-------7-------8-------
--------5-------5-------5-----|--------5-------5-------5-----
-----------5-------5-------5--|-----------5-------5-------5--
------------------------------|------------------------------
--0---------------------------|--0---------------------------
------------------------------|------------------------------
```

Thumb moves
to 5th string

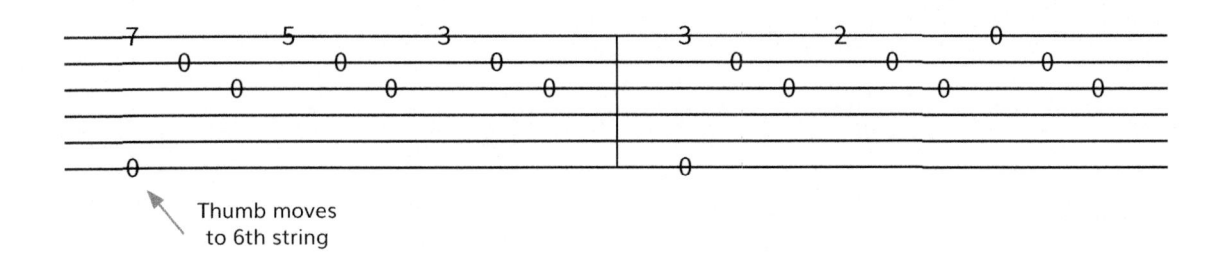

LESSON 10 | 107

Thumb moves to 6th string

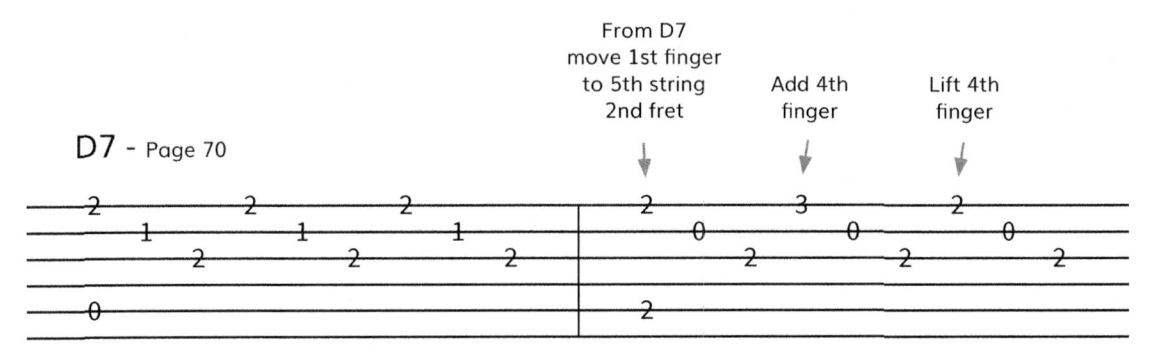

D7 - Page 70

From D7 move 1st finger to 5th string 2nd fret

Add 4th finger

Lift 4th finger

Thumb moves to 5th string

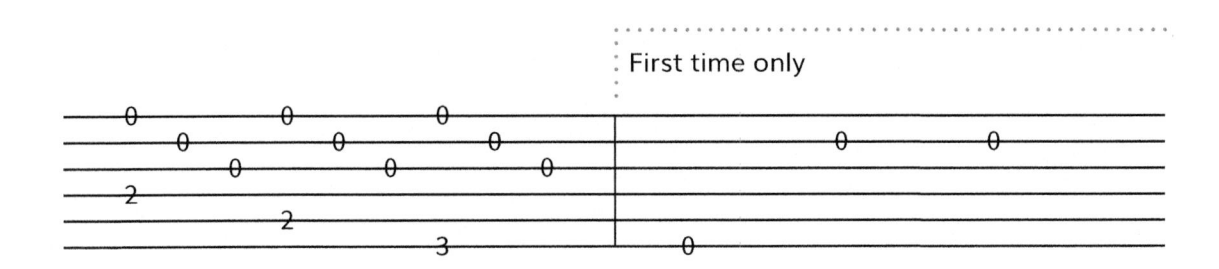

First time only

NOW GO BACK TO START

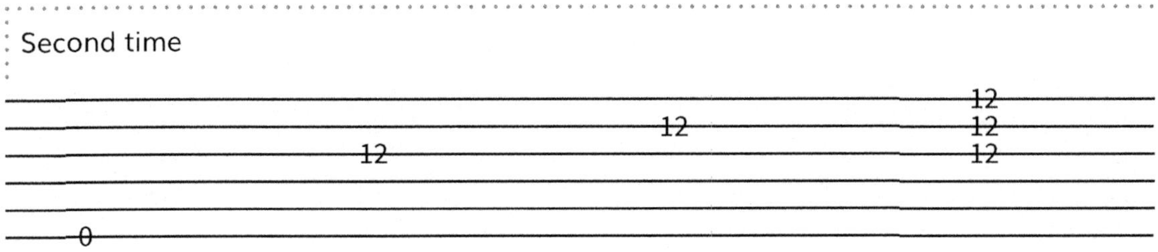

Second time

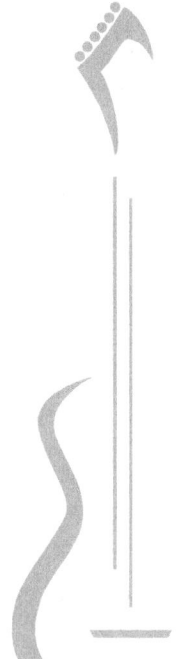

6 POPULAR FINGERSTYLES

Em - 48

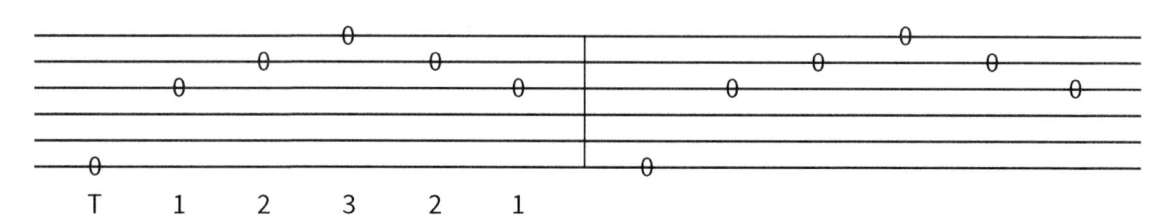

T 1 2 3 2 1

Am - 69

T 1 2 1 T 1 2 1

LESSON 10

Cmaj7 - 32

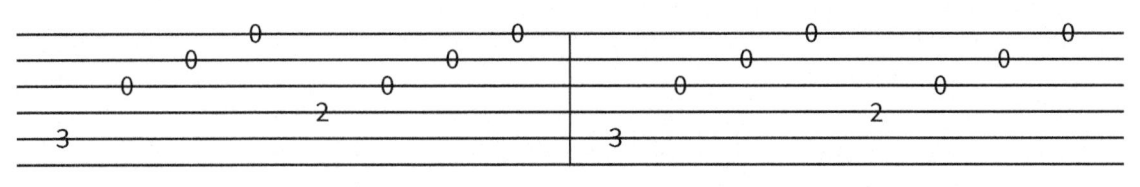

```
e|---------0-------------0-------|-------0---------0-------0-|
B|-----0-------0-----0-------0---|-----0-------0-------0-----|
G|---0-------------0-------------|---0-------------0---------|
D|-----------2-------------------|-------------2-------------|
A|-3-----------------------------|-3-------------------------|
E|-------------------------------|---------------------------|
   T   1   2   3   T   1   2   3
```

Asus2 - 64

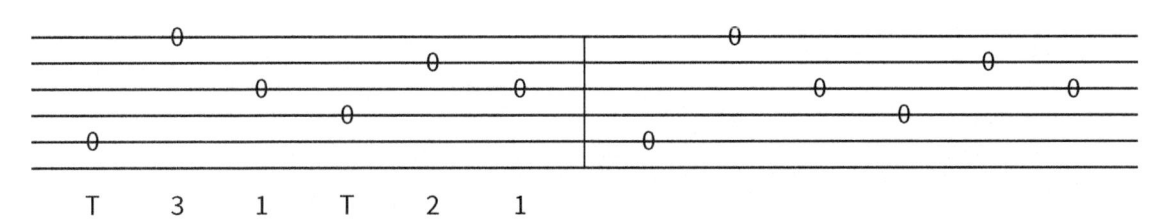

```
e|-------0-----------------------|-------0-------------------|
B|---0-------0-------0-----------|-----------0-----------0---|
G|-------------0-----------------|---0-----------0-----------|
D|-------------------------------|-0-------------------------|
A|-0-----------------------------|---------------------------|
E|-------------------------------|---------------------------|
   T   3   1   T   2   1
```

Cmaj7 - 32

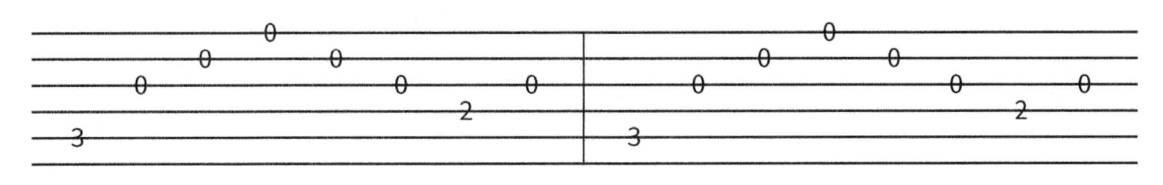

```
e|---------0---------------------|-------0-------------------|
B|-----0-------0---------0-------|-----------0---0-------0---|
G|---0-------------0-------------|---0---------------0-------|
D|-----------------2-------------|-----------------2---------|
A|-3-----------------------------|-3-------------------------|
E|-------------------------------|---------------------------|
   T   1   2   3   2   1   T   1
```

Am - 69

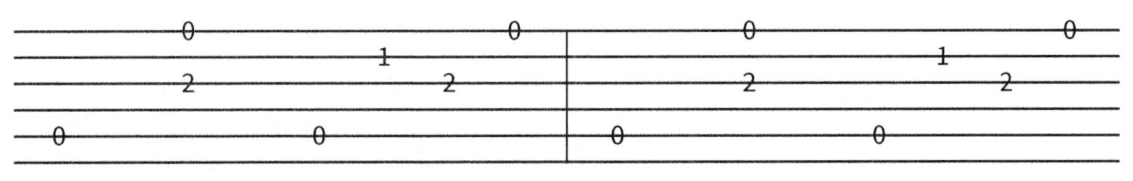

```
e|-------0-----------0-----------|-------0-----------0-------|
B|-----------1-----------1-------|-----------1-----------1---|
G|-----2---------2-------2-------|-----2-------2-------2-----|
D|-0-------0---------0-----------|-0-------0-----------------|
A|-------------------------------|---------------------------|
E|-------------------------------|---------------------------|
   T   1   T   1   T   1
       T
```

LESSON 10

50 MOST PLAYED GUITAR CHORDS

50 Guitar Chords | 111

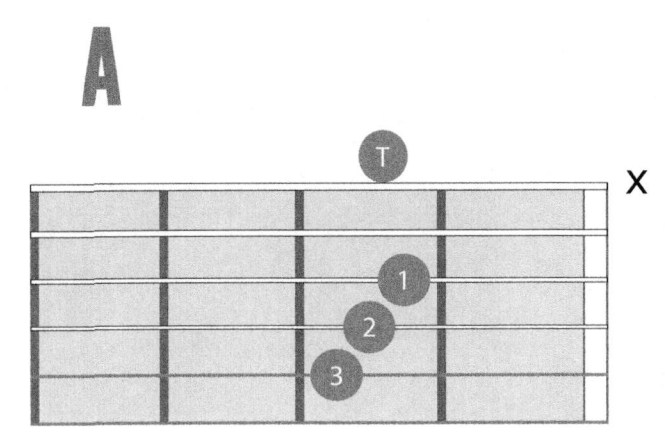

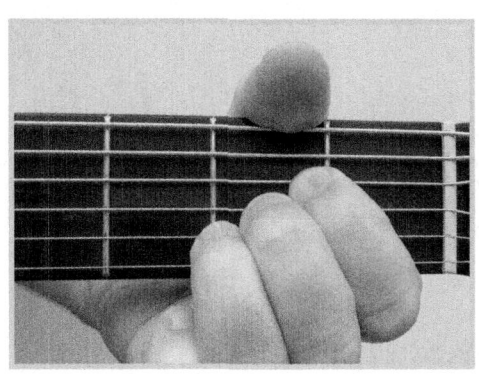

A

Asus2

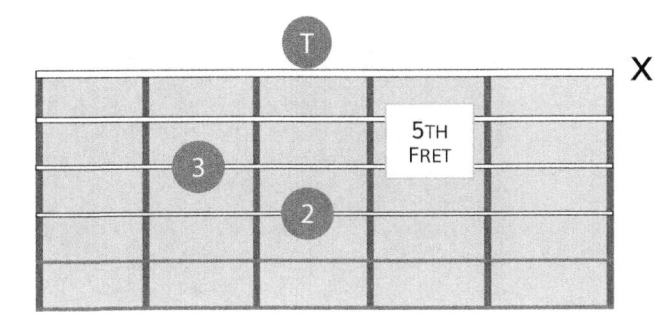

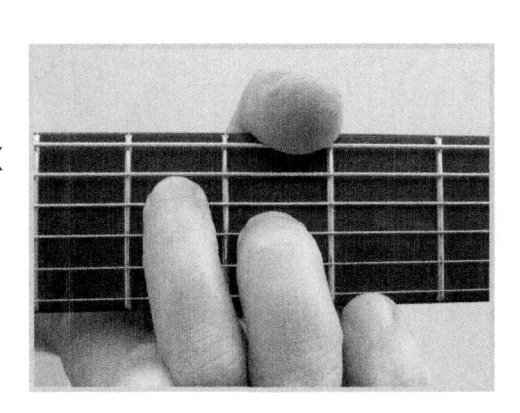

5th Fret

Amaj7

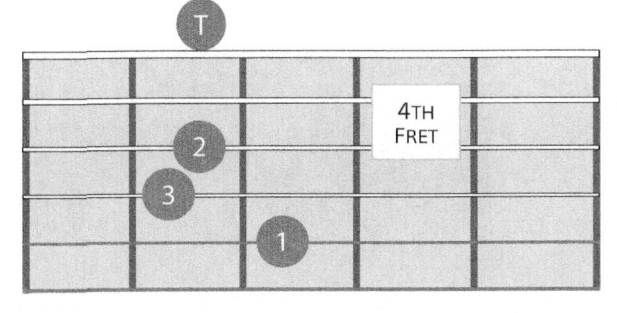

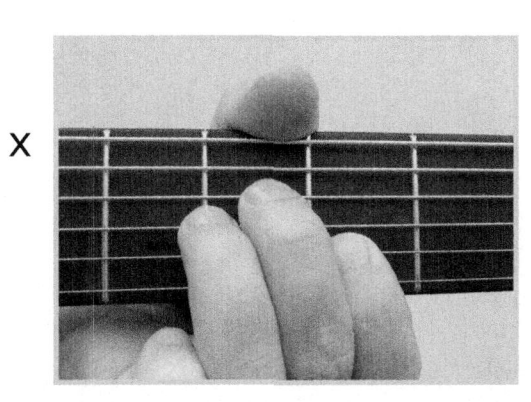

4th Fret

50 Guitar Chords | 112

A7

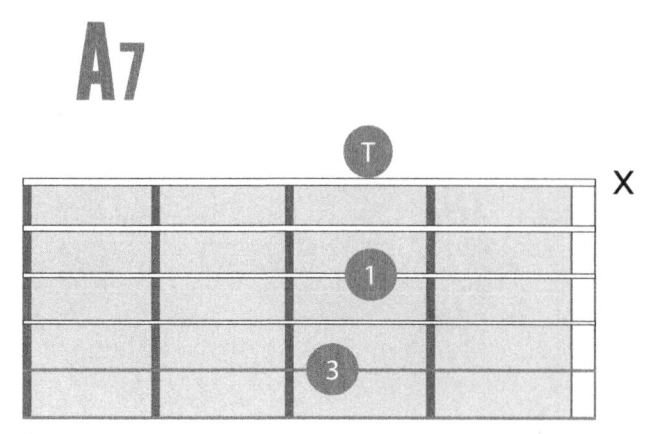

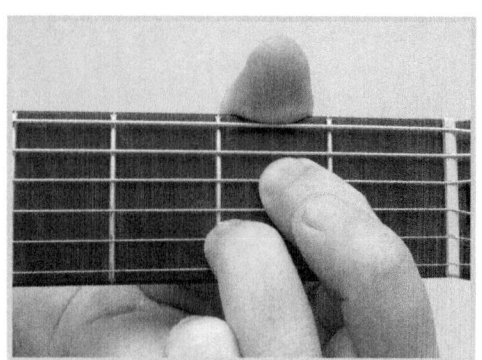

Am

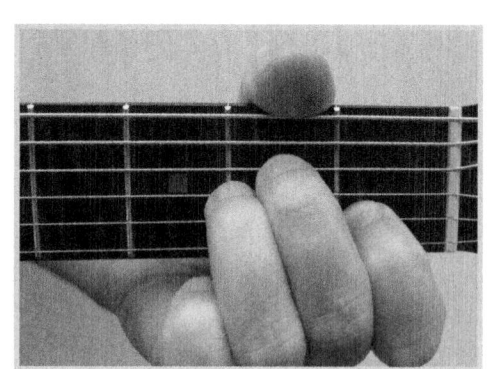

Am7

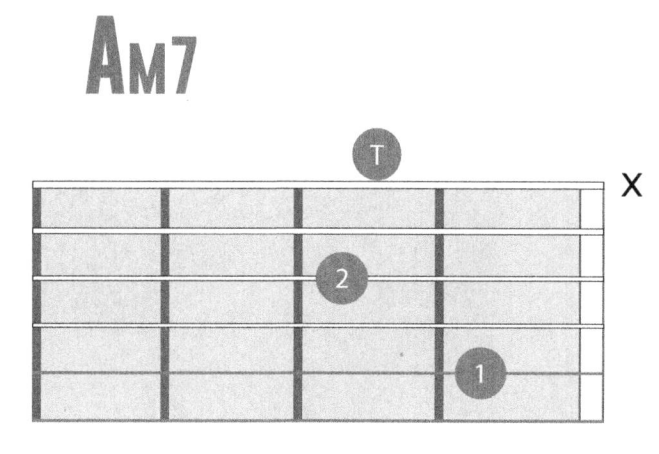

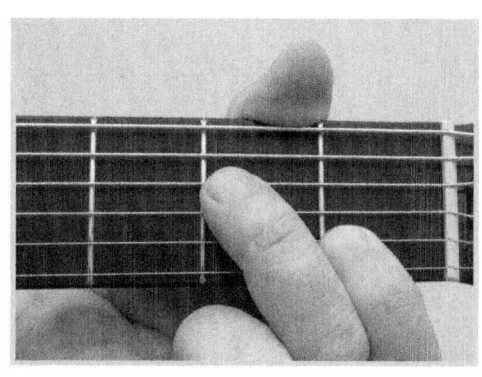

A/E

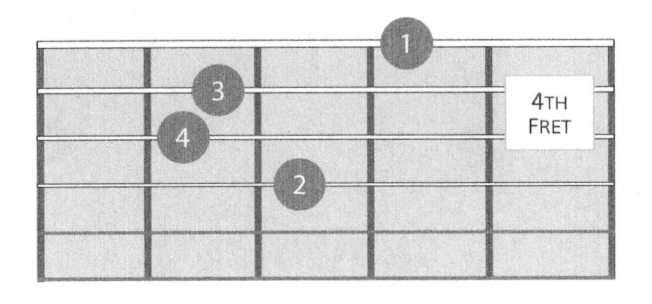

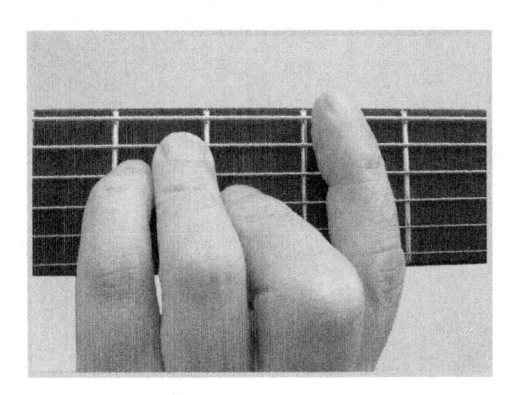

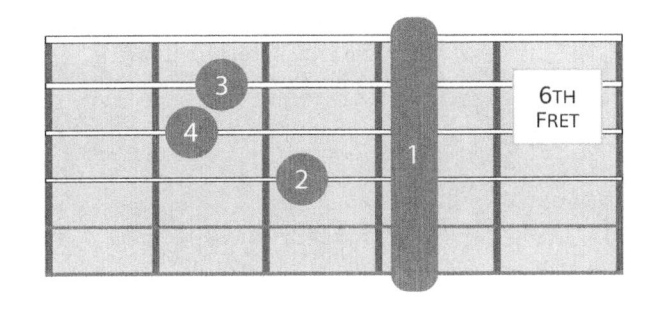

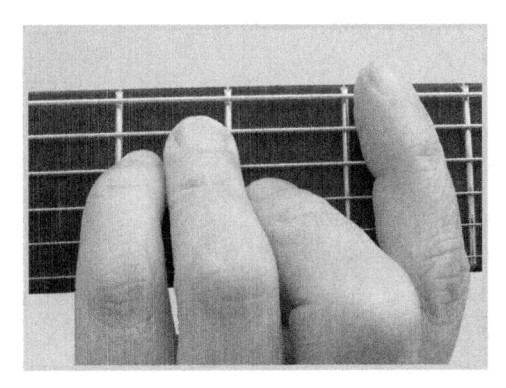

4TH FRET

B

6TH FRET

B *EASIER*

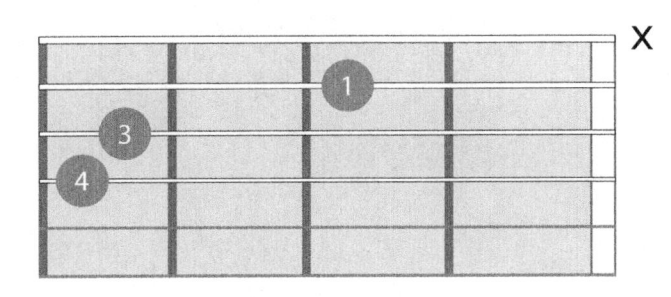

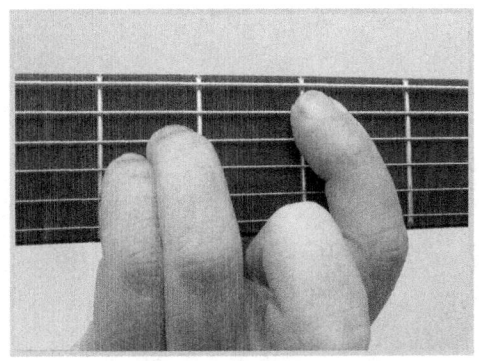

x

Bsus4

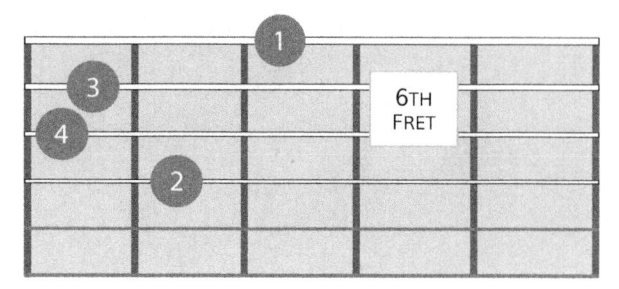

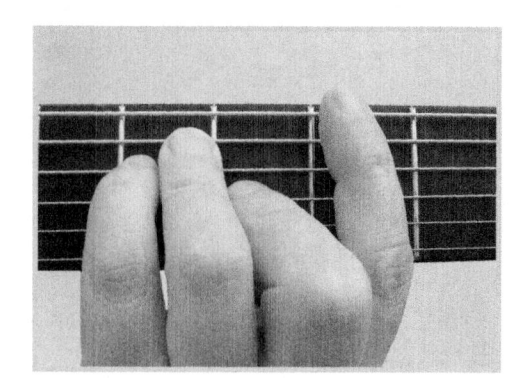

6TH FRET

Bm

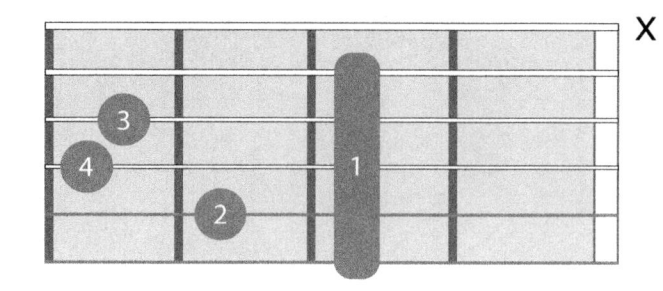

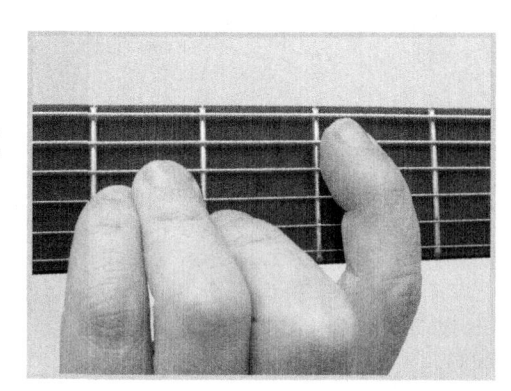

Bm *EASIER*

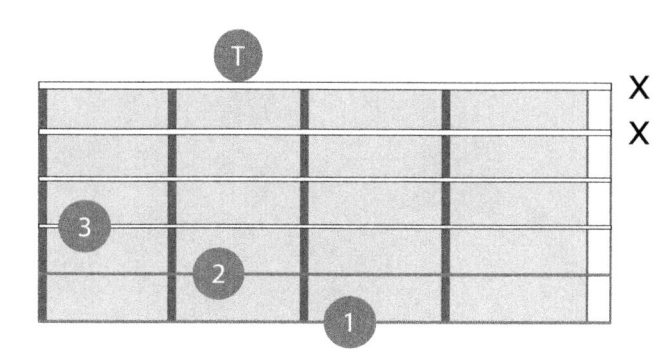

50 Guitar Chords

50 Guitar Chords | 115

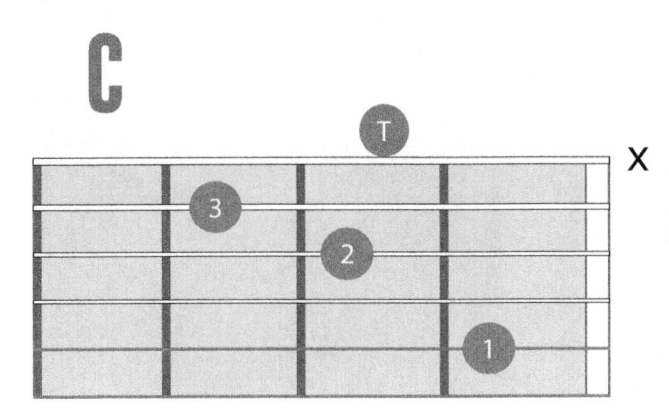

C

C ANOTHER WAY

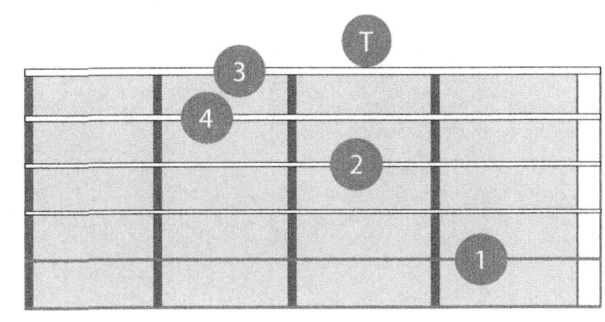

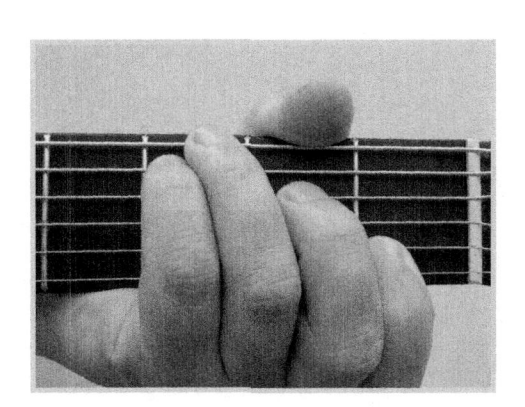

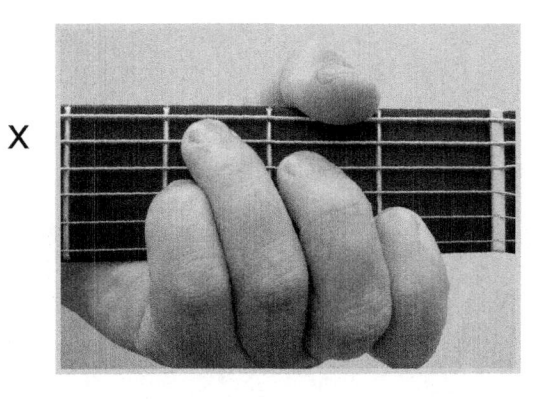

C7

50 Guitar Chords | 116

Csus4

Cmaj7

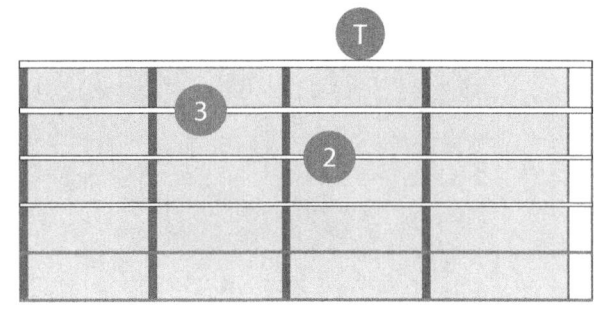

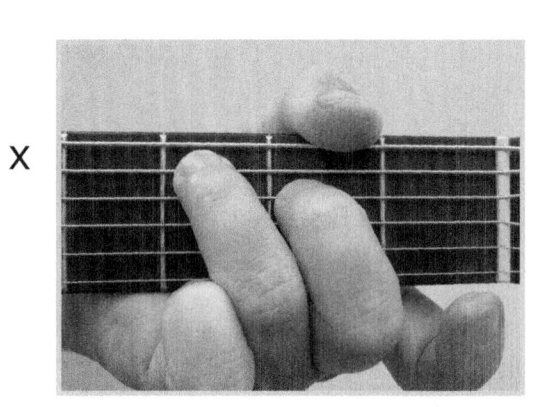

Cadd9

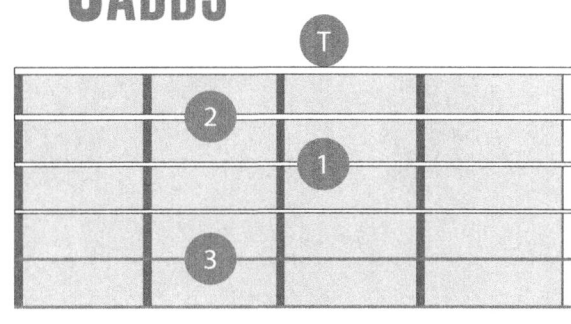

C/B

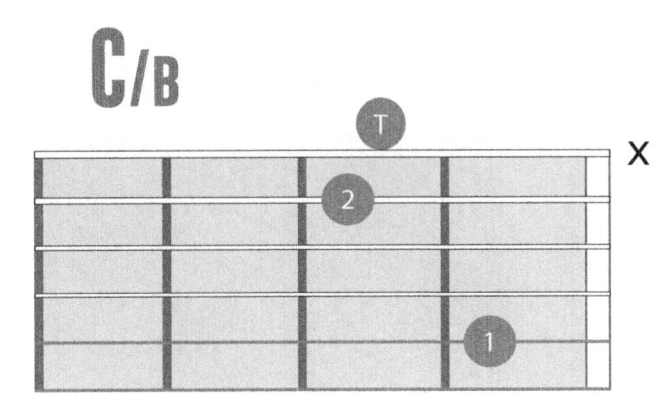

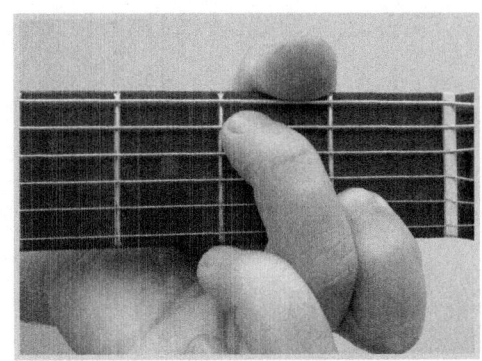

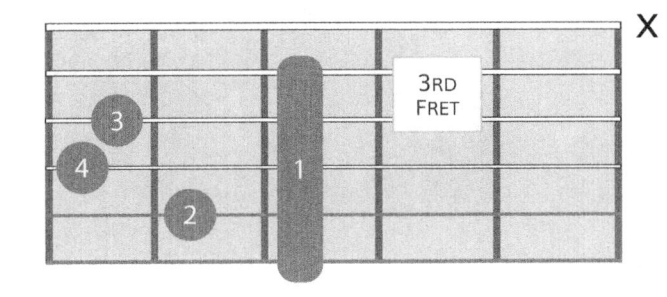

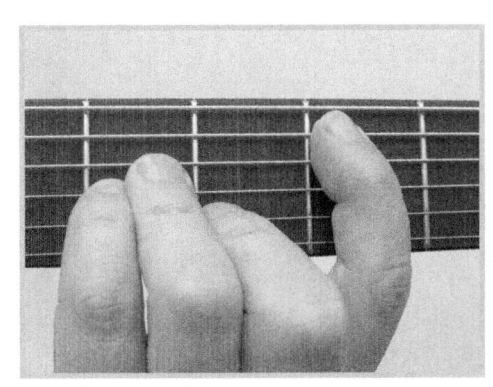

C#m

3rd Fret

C#m *EASIER*

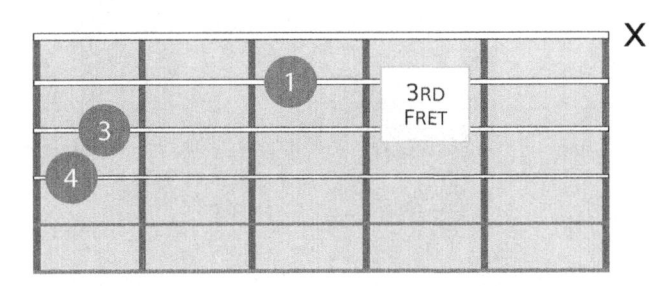

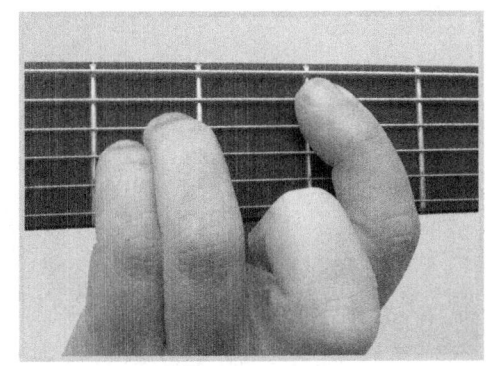

3rd Fret

50 Guitar Chords

50 Guitar Chords | 118

D

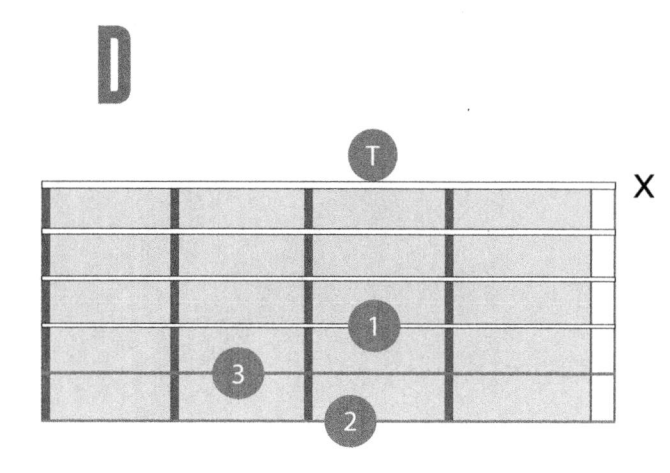

Dm

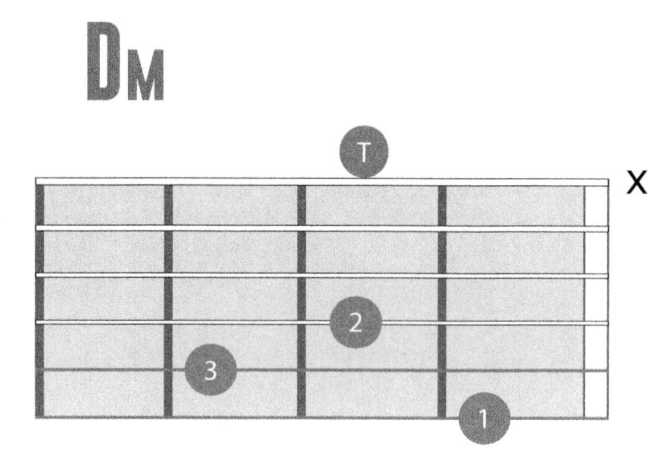

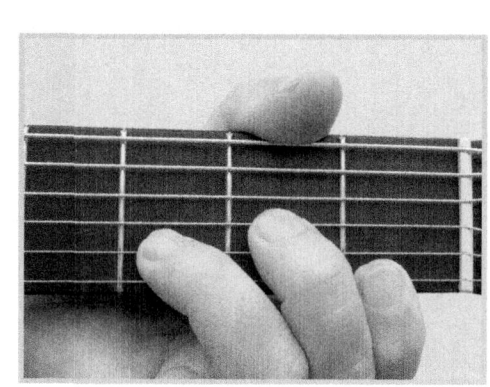

D7

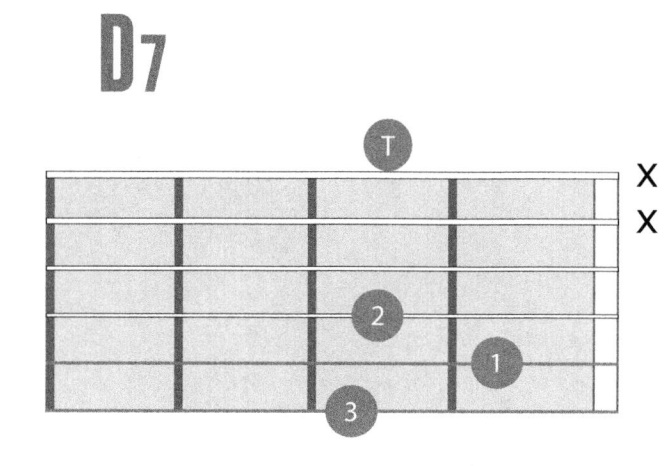

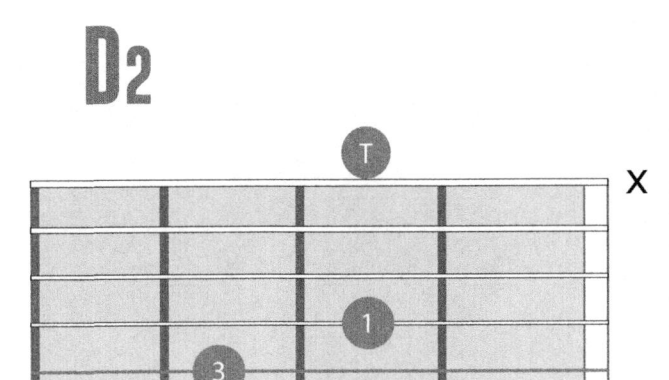

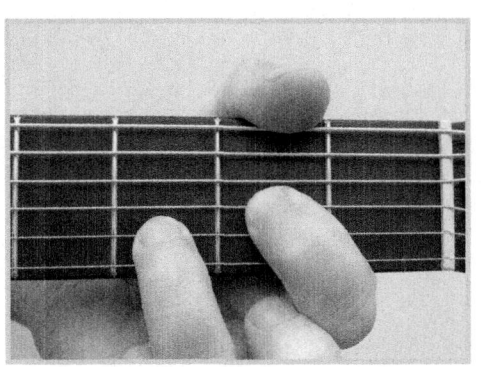

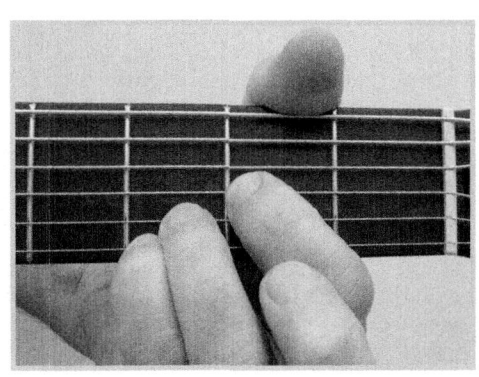

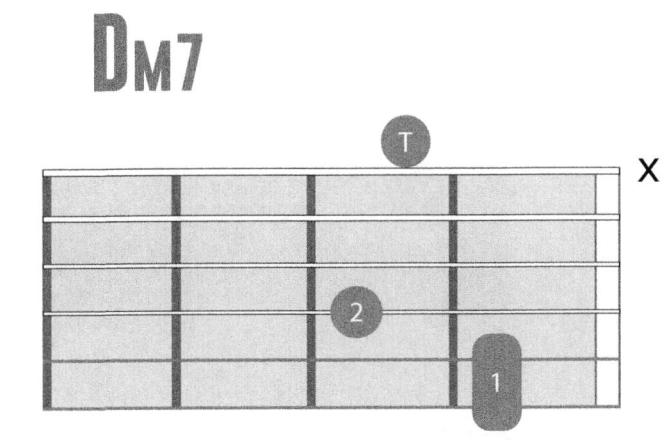

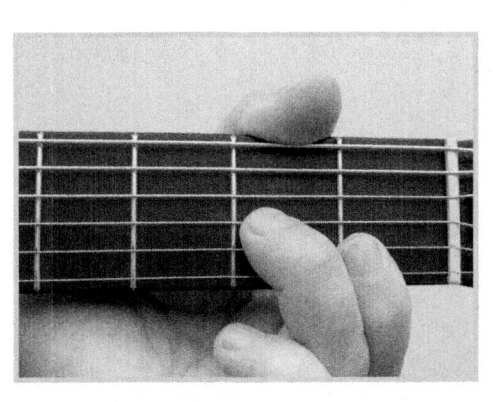

D2

Dsus4

Dm7

50 Guitar Chords | 120

Dmaj7

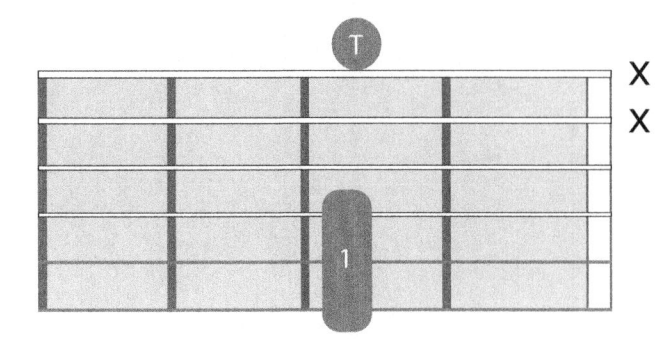

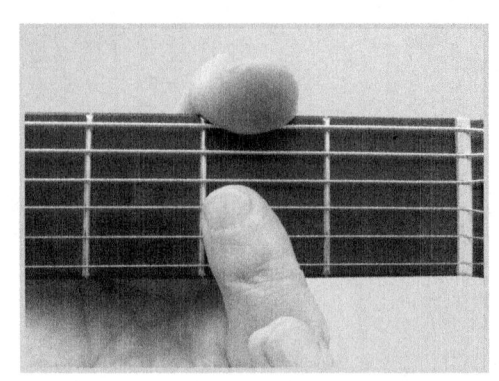

E

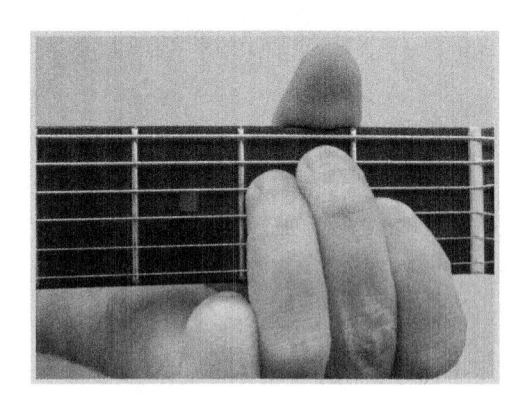

E/A POLYCHORD

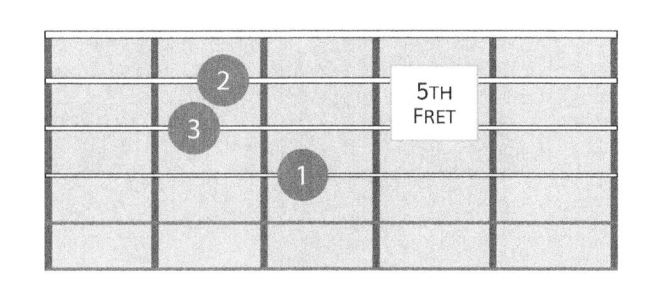

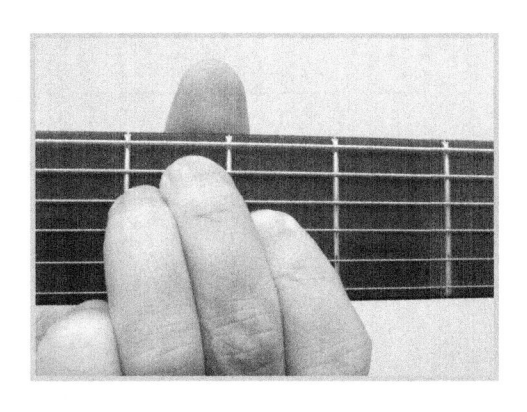

5TH FRET

E/B *POLYCHORD*

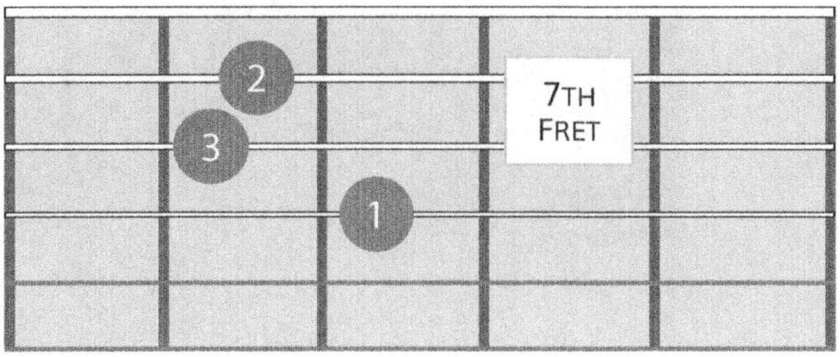

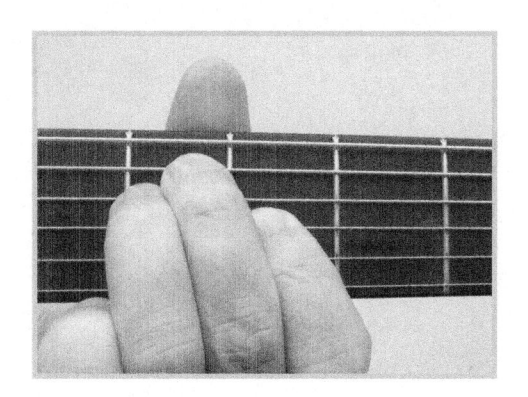

7TH FRET

Emaj7

3RD FRET

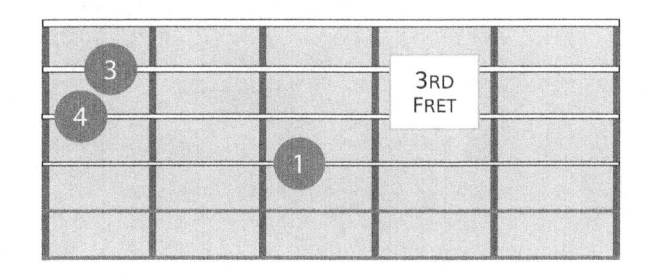

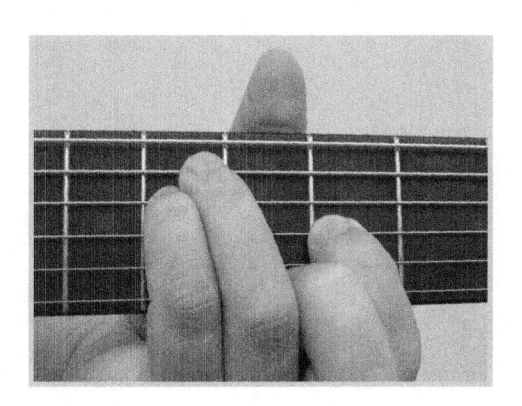

E7

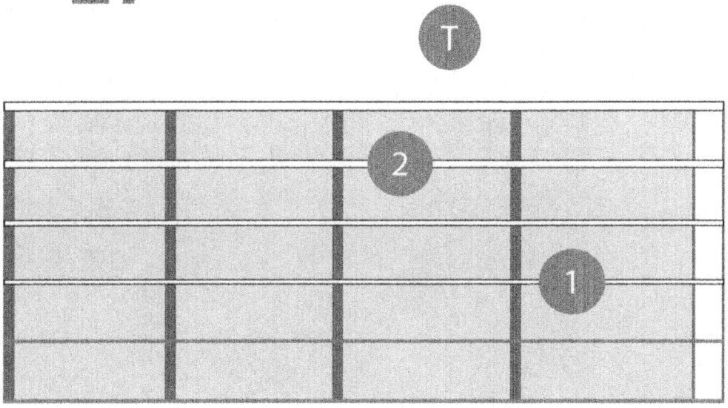

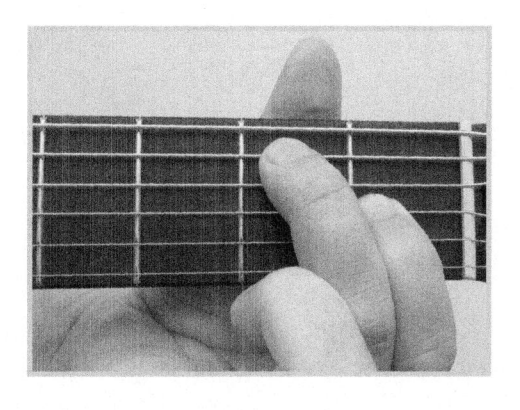

50 Guitar Chords

122

Esus4

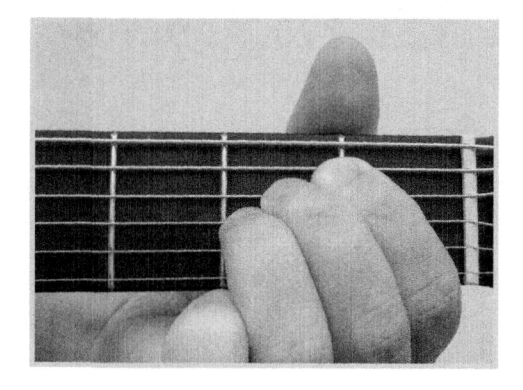

E5

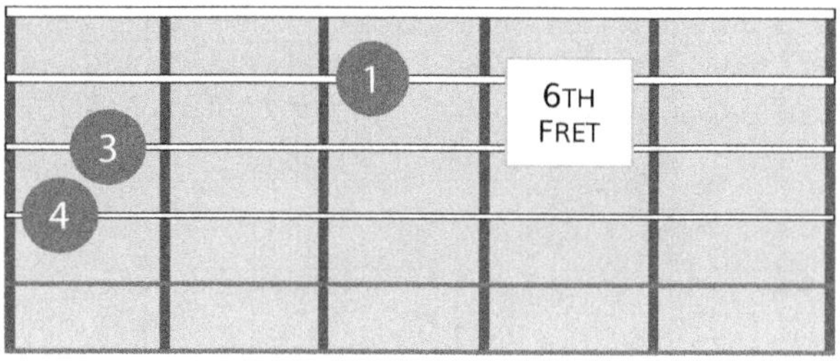

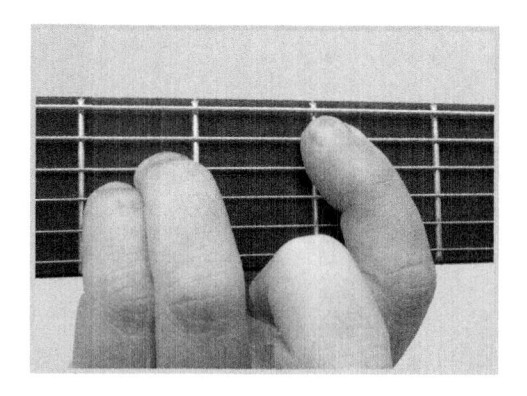

6TH FRET

Em/G

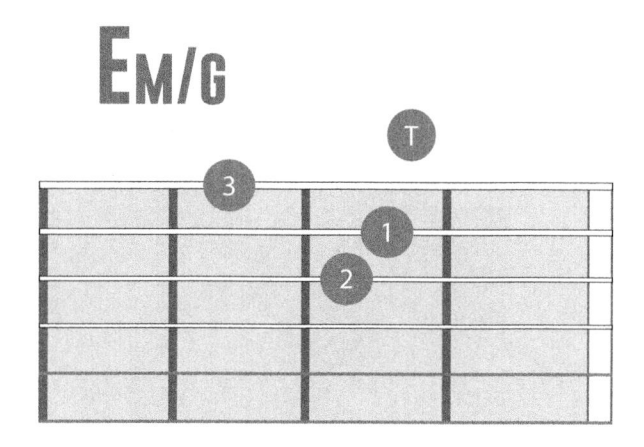

50 Guitar Chords

F

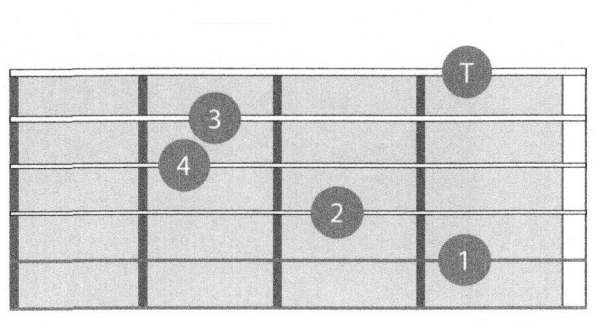

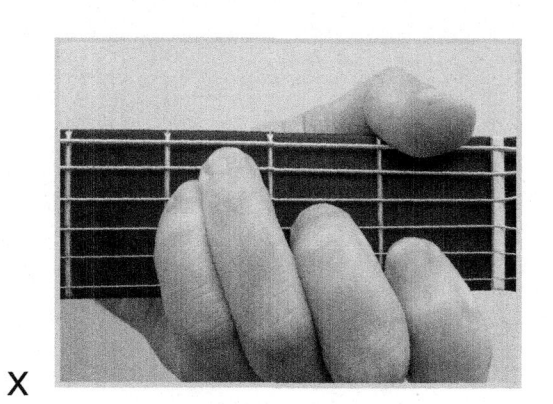

F *EASIER*

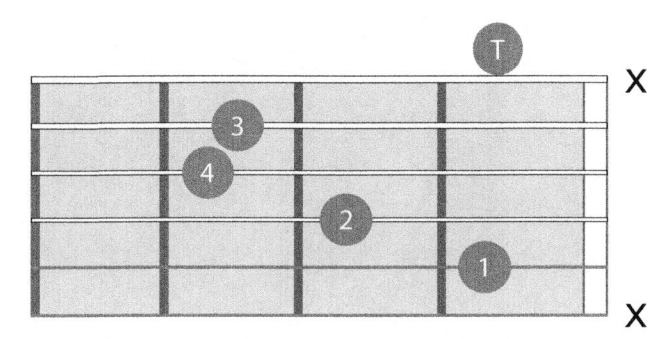

F2

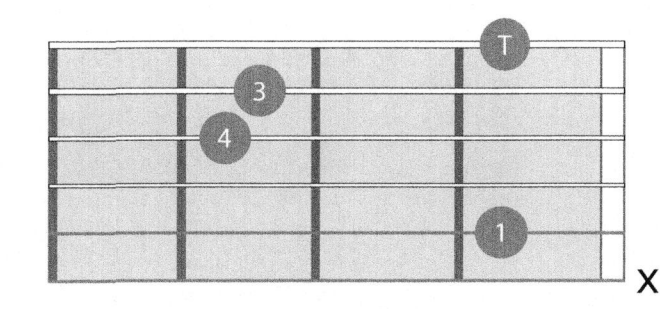

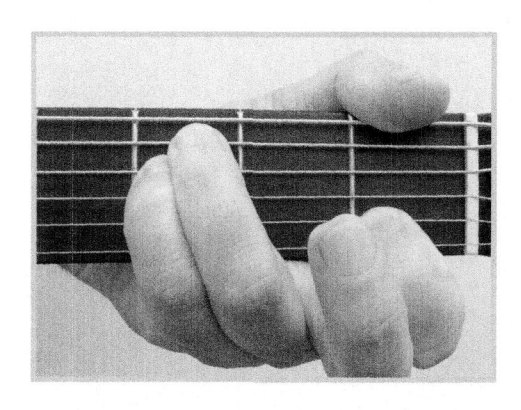

50 Guitar Chords | 124

Fmaj7

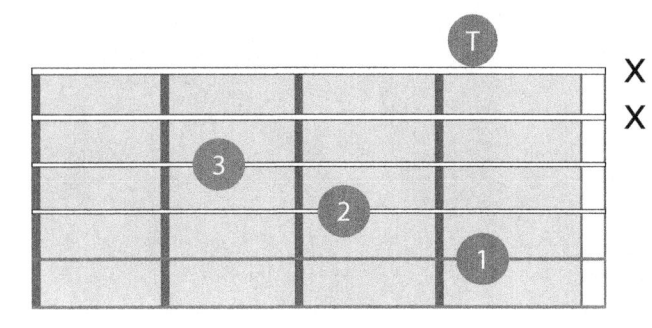

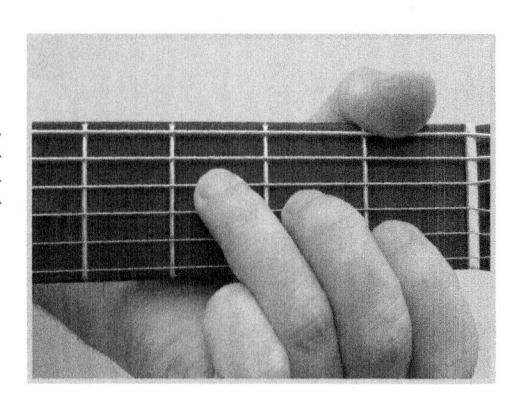

Fmaj7 *easier*

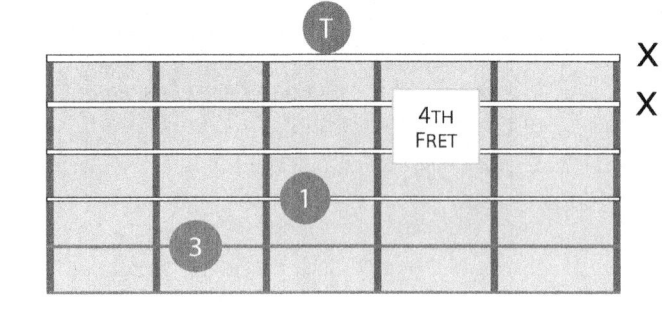

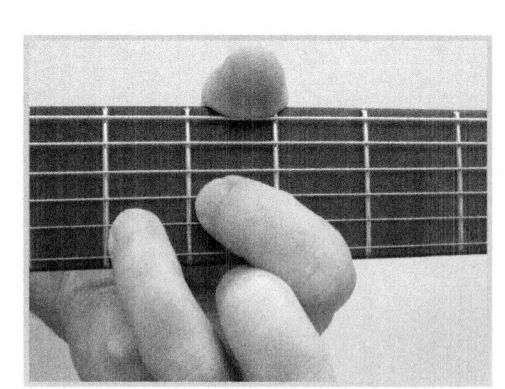

4th Fret

F#m7

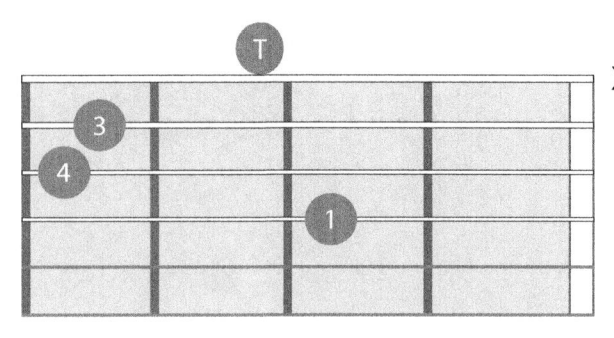

50 Guitar Chords | 125

F#m

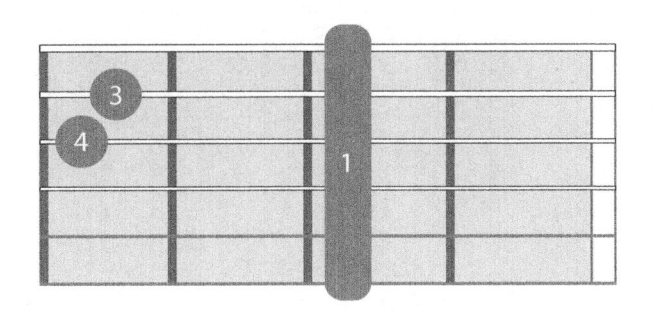

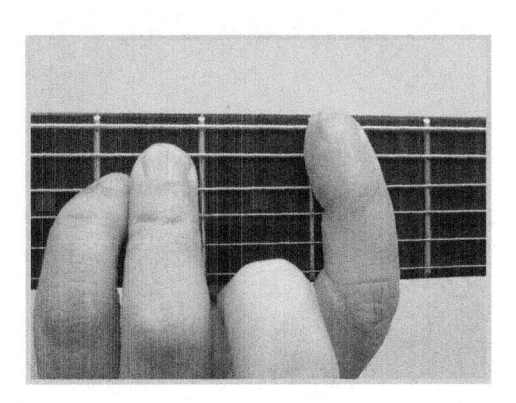

F#m *EASIER*

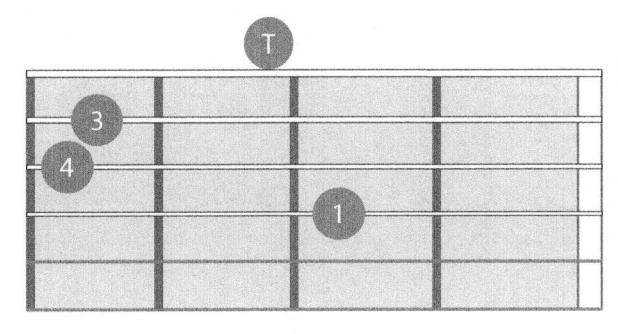

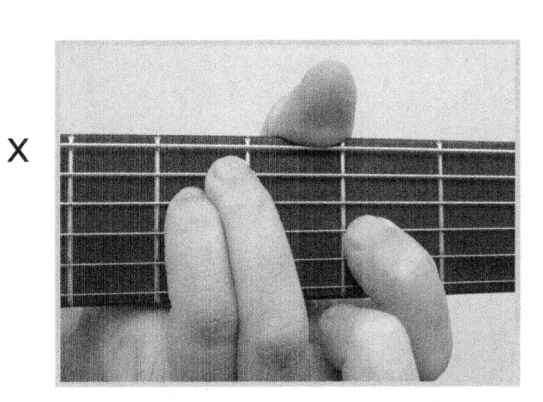

G

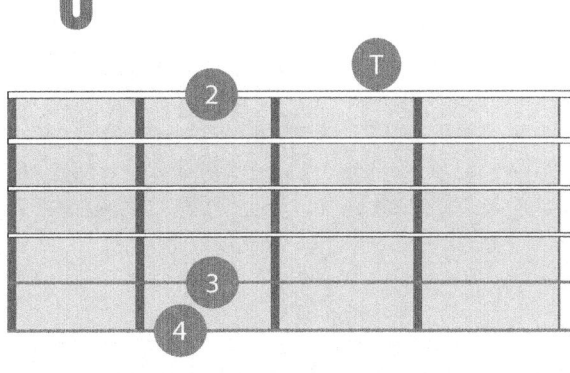

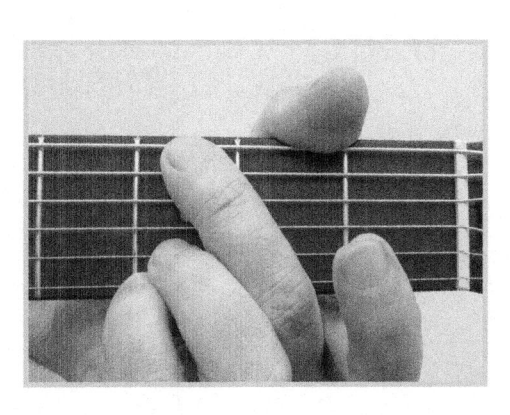

50 Guitar Chords | **126**

G ANOTHER WAY

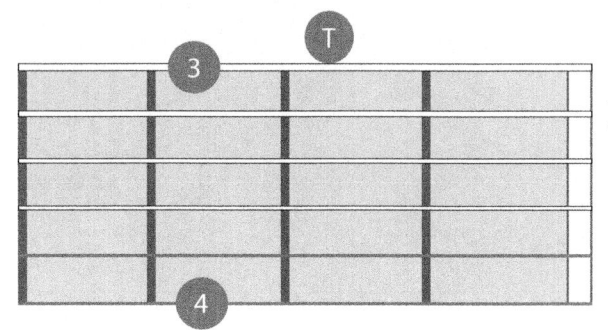

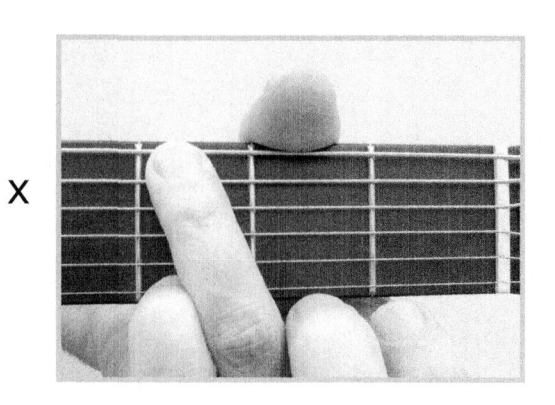

G7

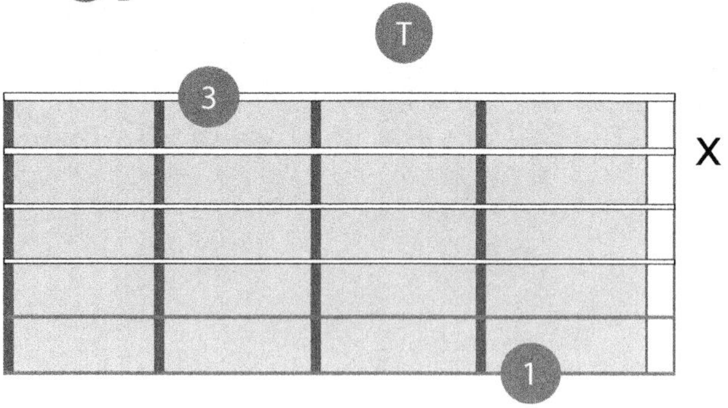

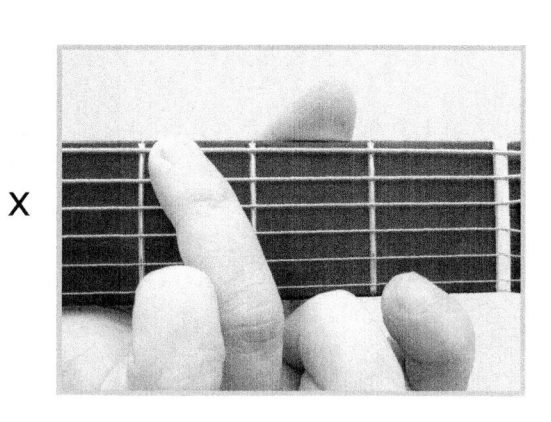

Gmaj7

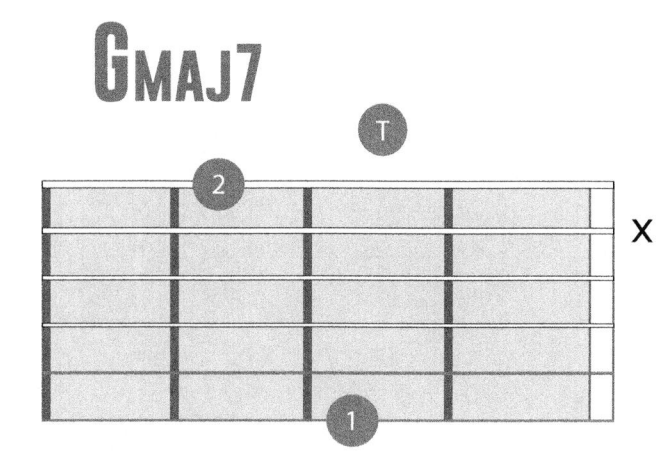

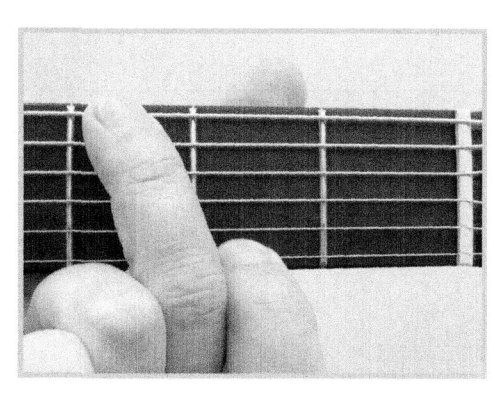

G addD7

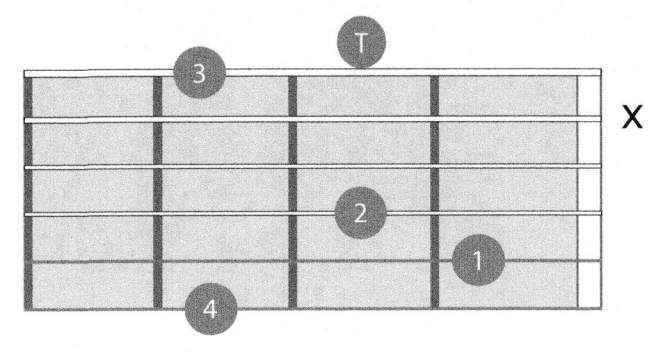

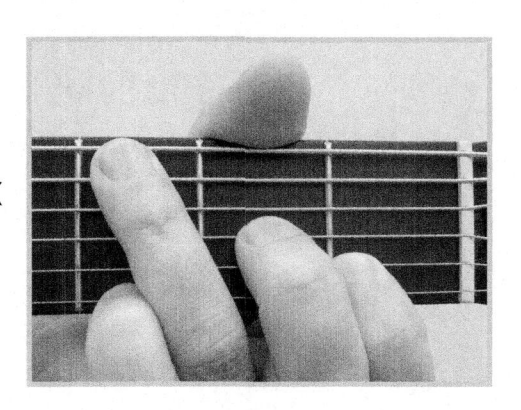

G sus4

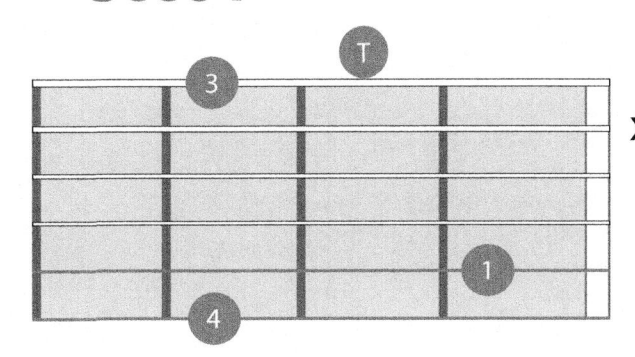

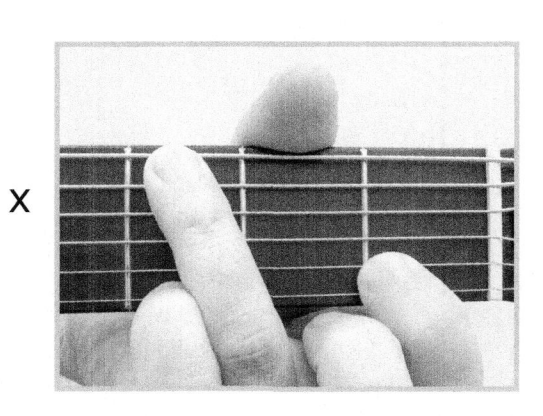

G addC

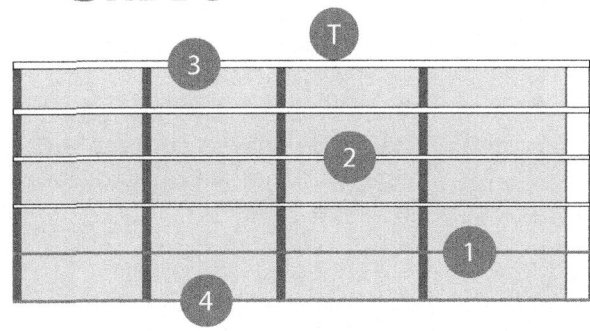

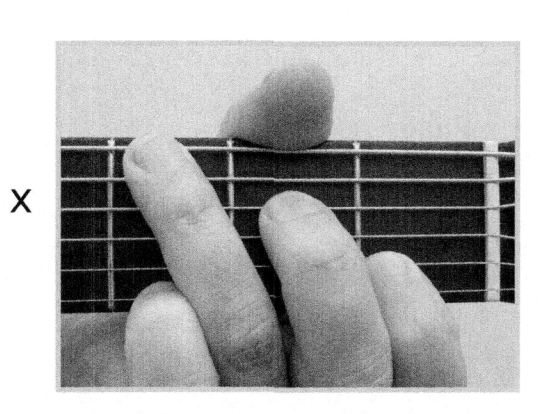

Have You Come This Far Step By Step?
If So ... You Have Done A Great Job!

CONGRATULATIONS!

Now You Can Play Guitar

Even if you have not fully mastered every lesson you're still doing very well. Any new discipline can be painful, but only for a short time.

It does get easier. The most important thing right now is to understand these lessons. In time they become a permanent part of your playing style.

And you have enough guitar chords, rhythms and playing skills for a lifetime of enjoyment.

Questions or Thoughts

Email

support@pauricmather.com

I would love to hear from you.

Review Request

If you have a moment, please leave a review. Your feedback greatly helps all of us on our musical journey.

MEET THE AUTHOR

Pauric Mather's ground breaking guitar books and lessons are truly unique. Easily the most individual and personalised you will ever find. They have helped thousands of people to learn guitar. What's even more remarkable is that you need no knowledge of music to learn from his teaching style.

As well as being an expert guitar teacher, Pauric Mather is the author of 4 #1 best sellers.

From Dublin, Ireland, he's been a professional guitarist since 1987, and has worked with many successful artists.

Pauric Mather is now the most translated guitar author in the world. His books and teaching methods are available in more than 10 languages.

LIVE WEBINAR - VIDEO - EMAIL SUPPORT

For all students learning from Pauric Mather guitar books.
Ask questions about anything you need help with.

Email support@pauricmather.com

Also By The Author

Printed in Great Britain
by Amazon